Invoking the
Warrior Spirit

Invoking the Warrior Spirit

New and Selected Poems

Tanure Ojaide

Africa World Press, Inc.

P.O. Box 1892
Trenton, NJ 08607

P.O. Box 48
Asmara, ERITREA

Africa World Press, Inc.

P.O. Box 1892
Trenton, NJ 08607

P.O. Box 48
Asmara, ERITREA

Copyright © 1999 Tanure Ojaide

First Printing 1999

Cover Art and Book Illustrations: Bruce Onobrakpeya
Book Design: Jonathan Gullery

This book is set in Clearface and Utopia

Library of Congress Cataloging-in-Publication Data

Ojaide, Tanure, 1948–
        Invoking the warrior spirit : new & selected poems / by Tanure
    Ojaide.
            p.   cm.
        ISBN 0-86543-710-6. -- ISBN 0-86543-711-4 (pbk.)
        1. Nigeria--Poetry. I. Title.
    PR9387.9.037315   1998
    821--dc21
                                                    98-41398
                                                      CIP

ACKNOWLEDGEMENTS ARE DUE TO
THE GREENFIELD REVIEW PRESS, LOTUS PRESS,
HEINEMANN (UK),
AND
MALTHOUSE PRESS THAT PUBLISHED THE COLLECTIONS
FROM WHICH THE SELECTIONS HAVE BEEN MADE.

Contents

Note: The poems are arranged in the order of their writing and not of publication. I have thus placed *The Endless Song* (1989) before *The Eagle's Vision* (1987) because though published later, it was completed before the latter.

I

Children of Iroko and Other Poems

(1973)

For my Grandmother, Amreghe,
and Chris Okigbo

MESSAGE OF LUST

I

TIGERS OWN the homes,
Where shall goats sleep;
Where shall travelling virgins sleep
In a village of lust?

Grave problems drive sleep away.
It is dawn and the virgins
Are not deflowered;
The goats are alive.

When the vulture came to the market
There was no food;
The coffin-seller is unhappy
Because there is no sale.
How can we be safe without
Carrying our heads in a strong shell?
How can our fortunes reach home
Without encountering armed robbers?

II

The fowl is guzzling corn,
It knows not for how much it is bought;
The cook is frying eggs,
He feels not the bruise of the hen's anus;
Soldiers are firing bullets into the crowd,
They will boast of those they have killed;
The Pay and Records boys are riding Yamaha,
They are paying and wrecking Nigeria.
Sadat and Sadek are threatening,
The recruits will fight the Israelis.

Recruits fight the war,
The world congratulates
And remembers the generals.

III

The giant marched through cassava farms,
And they say no plant was touched;
They will also shoot the chameleon
And deny they are oppressors, deny their guilt.

When shall wars end?
Diplomats don't know, the bedbug
Doesn't care for the taste of your blood.

CHILDREN OF IROKO

Now acolyte, you must dress new
In white calico with red bands,
Like the virgin priestess
A feather-hat from forest birds
And lead the procession on.

Carry them on:
Newly baked serrated chalk
A white cock without a crow
Three-lobed kolanuts
Seven half-pennies
Put them on the white plate, carry
Them on towards the happy shrine
And let the cow be led behind. . .

A year is gone past
After rains, harvests and suns.
Hair has gone more grey without
New entrance to the grave-fields.
Women have groaned, not for grief
But in begetting more sons.
And children are saved from pythons
And puff-adders.

Now is the new moon
Crescent favourable;
Dry tumulus at the right hand
Lacks libation wine to flourish.
He needs a cow, a milky cow
Send a herald to announce
       Protective prayers
       Fecundive rites
       And happy thanks. . .

Acolyte, the priestess by your right
Place the weighty carriage on the floor
And touch your forehead on the ground.
Pour the wine
  in drops;
       Let it stream
        over the ground
           to sink beneath
And let Osonobrughwe take his fill. . .
"You show you love us
We kneel before you and for you
We thank you."
Fast and fast, beat loud the drums
Back to begin a new year.

WHAT I CARRY ALONG

I

SLEEPING on a leopard's skin
Or sharing a lion's den as room-mate
Tremble not for fear in the jungle.
Only lightning reigns supreme—
The bamboo defies the skies, the palm burns
Under the angry laughter of the heavens.

II

WEALTH COMES and goes like cases at court
The riddling owl hoots to advantage today
Tomorrow the cry is blistering.

Last dry season, finding fertile farms
The dove filled its low stomach
Hovering happy antics before the sky.
Then came the rains, came the delta storms
So starved that it prepared to hang.
What fun, fellows?
Oil boasts: "For ever and ever
Shall I remain on top of water."
It shall come, rock salt shall come
To beat oil into profound loss.

III

THE HUNTER COMES home bagging a hawk
Enemies rejoice for the game
Their fowls are safe to increase their eggs
But a question for the fowlherd:
Is the hawk the only living
That doesn't wish the fowls to cluck?

IV

BULLETS HAVE STRUCK a captain
And enemies are happy
The cold has dispersed
And caught fishes in ponds.
The mourners heavy, enemies rejoice.

V

A POOR MAN is a soldier-ant
A soldier-ant he is
Rain brings life, sunshine death.
The poor man is like a kid
The sacrificial kid offered gods
To appease witches at crossroads
And bring peace to town.

In a war to enrich masters
Recruits die for majors to be promoted.

FOR CHRIS OKIGBO

TOMORROW ANOTHER POET shall die in the
    battle-field
Tomorrow a prophet shall be smashed by
    a clap of thunder
Tomorrow the crowded streets shall be silent. . .

Create a place for us in the grove
Create a place for mourners in the grove
For the town-crier is dead, Idoto's son is gone
Okigbo's a skull . . .

We shall dance with rattles
And with drums; the rhythm shall be solemn.
Leave us dance and be danced for
Let us sing and be sung for
Okigbo's a skull . . .

From the tower of nibs
The weaverbird twittered in the nest
A nest which was no citadel for a reader
Turned marksman for profane humanity;
He's become a skull. . .

Tomorrow the crowded streets shall be silent
For he went into silence himself ringing the bells;
The darkness that ate him standing
    in the path of thunder.

From the ancients to *Tee Es*, from East to West
He quarried deep for his sophisticated mansion
Some quarrelled he never asserted darkness
Others called him a pickpocket he proudly
    accepted
And when the clap of thunder came, the prodigal
Embraced the clap, was clapped by thunder.

Pour oil on him who is silent
Scatter flowers for him who was silenced
Crown him silenced in the front with palm
Light a candle for the dead
For he who is silent, he who was silenced
Ended for us daily forgetting our childhood
Wrote for us daily inking sheets for humanity;
Chris Okigbo's gone. . .

        (December, 1970)

FEBRUARY 1ST OFFERING

(for Kunle Adepeju of U.I.)

WHEN WINDOWS BREAK and teargas
Infects the air the body jumps for action
When noise caresses the air when stones fly
The body jumps for action
When the land blushes for pristine rights
The body goes into action. . .

Drums and stones fondle the body
Speech and faces fondle the body
Fondle the body to excitement
Drive the body to action
The ram in the foreground
Invited by the cry of action
Invited by the call for offering

The moment of it that crowns
Hero and martyr
Dances Death the unknown summoner
Dances Death the famished self-seeker
Dances the summoner the dismal step

And then came the push, the struggle. . .
Cry of action calls the hero
Death patronizes the martyr
And the offering the offering
To the ram the bullet
And violence, violence

Then the hero knows not the hero
The martyr knows not the martyr
And after the last march of the dance
The man that jumped for action
IN MEMORIAM . . .

THE CURSE

I

WHO PAYS EXAMINATION questions for dowry
Who donates an undeserved "A" to his mistress
The scorpion's bitterest venom confuse the don's
    brains
Sango's strongest bolt smash the don's brains

II

Who parades an intellectual but only a fraud
The sturdiest cobra spit into his peering eyes
Sango and Amadiora burn his gowns
Ogun's heaviest rod lash his flat buttocks

III

Who smiles for a plagiarized paper well-read
Who tattles to be heard for a wit
The bees make thorough grimace of his joy
Chukwu's smallpox uglify his elevated face
The liveliest bug enervate his hours of rest
Olokun, weigh him down to the bottom of waters.

II

Labyrinths
of the Delta

(1986)

For Anne and Angela

A camel is dear at a penny if you
    do not need a camel.
A single word is cheap at a thousand gold
    pieces,
      if it is essential to you.
          —Idries Shah, *Thinkers of the East.*

And there was a dark exultation
in sacred things torn apart,
and, bitter as wormwood, this passion
was a wild delight to my heart.
          —Alexander Blok, "The Muse."

from LABYRINTHS OF THE DELTA

II

Let us go to the River
With drums, goats, and cowries;
Let us go, draped in our favourite madras,
Powdered and perfumed;
Let us go to her.
She called us this way,
And we came, absorbing accents
Into our tongue.

O Water Bride
Moving without a boat in deep waters,
You heeded the anguished cries of our souls,
Ferried us fugitives across the midstream torrents;
You made us calabashes on the water
And delivered us on the bank, giving us
The virgin beauty of the Delta.
Who until now in a clear voice
Told us we had a place,
And we had been running in the dark
From the cat's eyes of our tormentors?
        We thank you,
But what words can fully tell the depth
Of our feelings? Your name on our lips,
Eternal glory to the Bride.

III

You stood here, waiting since the beginning of
    time,
O Soil to give yourself to us, and here we are.

When we came to the irokos, we saw ourselves in
    full light,
And grew taller by several fingers.
We tasted the first laughter of our adult lives
And knew we had arrived at our God-built home.
At the River with a thousand branches we downed
What remained of a bare existence—
We brought along Aridon, our memory,
And Uhaghwa, our voice for songs.

Let daily rain beat our heads—
We have had so much drought
That we would sleep in rain.

The iguana ran to us like a god to his people,
We offered it eggs to remain our friend.
The ogbodu bird ran here and there on stilts—
So much grace in the party that welcomed us.

We did not fall from the sky, we did not
Pop out of holes. Our first home was northern,
And we had lived there from the time man set foot
On the earth. It was beyond the hot sands—
We crossed a thousand frontiers to be ourselves.
In our flight a god-usurping man tantalized us
    with security

In a walled town, and bound some of us for sacri-
    fice
To dreamed-up gods.
A thousand frontiers we came through,
Each with its own torments.

    Come and dance
    It is here we dance
    Come and dance
    It is on this land we dance
    Come and dance
    It is on this soil we dance

IV

Before God's praisenames were peddled
    about in a platter,
The Delta was one region:
A tropical garden where you picked for free
Whatever appealed to your constitution.
The land carried people on its back, proffering
    bounties.
The sea opened its mouth, a watchdog at the gate,
And into it Urhiapele found its way, glittering,
Paraded by mermaids, acolytes of love.
Streams ran through the landscape,
And the world stood on firm feet:
Irokos, mahoganies, the earth's props.
With the sun life was an invaluable gift
Wrapped in green foliage.

When God became everyone's flag and mask,
Conquistadors drove gunboats from the Atlantic,
Crossed the air, destroyed the foetuses spawning
    in wombs,
And opened up the land into whitelaced shrines.
They drove stakes into the labyrinths of the Delta,
    fearing
They would wander into cannibalistic snares.
Then flashing gold at our faces, broke our love,
And split the fold into liveried bands.

    Turn the tortoise back, O Waters,
    Bring him back
    Spare him mishap on the way
    Bring him back to me;
    He broke not only my hands
    But also my legs and ribs;
    Bring him back to me
    Spare him mishap on the way here
    And let the villain taste
    What he inflicted on me
    From my own hands.

V

The River swells with boats, a regatta for state-
    hood,
And throughout the land a warriors' dance
    at homecoming.
The task is done, and we mark the victory;
Our sweat is no more of hardship but mirrors of
    joy.

In the thronged assembly, gods and men:
Uhaghwa in a feather-hat singing of the love we
    owe the land;
Abadi, axe in hand; Egba with his leonine dog;
And in our midst numerous deities,
    some unheard of
But bearing our names.
    They have come back, the dead,
Moved by our thumping feet, voices, and drums:
For his dedication, Kwokori will be our main
    street;
May Essi's matchet no longer be raised
    against neighbours
But against robbers of the new-found home;
Mowarin, my namesake, telling us great things
    are coming;
Okitiakpe, singing and dancing as no man has
    ever done;
And thousands—the couriers whose blood was
    libation abroad—
They have come to the concourse, happy spirits.

Uvo! Ogidigbo! Your names will endure
    like the sky.
After you were driven through half the world,
    you stood
Your ground and beat back your foes—
    ama hirhe erherie!
Not once did you go to battle without returning
    with spoils.
O you warriors, give us the resolve to fight for
    years on years

In the security of your shield of leaves.

Come and dance
It is here we dance
Come and dance
It is on this land we dance
Come and dance
It is on this soil we dance.

DEATH OF THE WARRIOR

(for Ramat)

The storm blew away the stars from the sky
And drowned us in our own tears

The giant who burrowed through hilly land to
        water
And knew the hidden chant
That would redeem us from a curse
Ran into a storm and fell in the street

The storm blew away our light
And drowned us in our own tears

He who blew pepper and smoke into the lion's
        face
And made the beast run into a trap
(We clapped our hands for a great one)
Was struck in early morning light

The storm blew away our pride
And drowned us in our own tears

The door that shielded us
Is torn off
And our home is exposed
To serpents and robbers

The storm blew away the stars from the sky
And drowned us in our own tears

The son who gave us direction
Is forever gone
He did not live to walk with a stick
But covered more than a lifetime's strides

The storm blew away the stars from the sky
and drowned us in our own tears

Consolers tell me
The warrior is gone
His lieutenant lives
The stump grows back to the same tree

The storm blew away the pride of the forest
And drowned us in our own tears

His inheritor
Will be pelted with taunts
If the promise is abandoned
To rot at the wayside

The storm blew away the stars from the sky
And drowned us in our own tears.

FOR MY CHILD IN HOSPITAL

When the breath-wresting hyena stole to your bed
in its meanness, your angels were up,
and they drove it back by turning you into a scare-
    crow.
I thought my puppy had strayed into a
    diabolic rut,
deaf to my loud whistle. In another minute,
you would have shed your childhood
for an ancestral veil, beside Granny,
and left me a wretched soul in double agonies.

You would have gravely erred, for no rams
would empty their throats to fill your thirst,
and you would be a mendicant forever
since only those whose waists cropped a homeful
enjoy their final passage . . .

For once your teeth clench, not in jest of
    Superman,
but as you wear bilboes in your bones,
    crisis-ridden;
your tears mirror a gash too deep for your thin
    years.
If it could be shared, your mummy and I would
    relieve you;
for you deserve a playground,
not this grim shadow covering your sunlight.
You live on a haunted frontier,
and every day is grace enough to fashion an escape.

Decades ago my mother counted seven or more
    mounds
in the backyard before she slept, belly down.
By then the beast came in witches' masks,
owls with neighbours' voices;
she could not tell what bit, stung, or tore her
    young ones
despite her watchful eyes; she saw nothing.

When the hyena slipped back into our midst,
we threw our drums into kitchen-racks, cut the
    nightly dance
for vigil. This violation has brought us an anglo-
    indian shaman,
who is telling us about tomorrow: *Tomorrow you
    shall*
see more battles, but celebrate today's victories;
perhaps by tomorrow you shall be better armed. . .
Even as she talks, you call my name;
and now, the erstwhile threatening sky is all stars.
The drums invite us to new steps.

A VERDICT OF STONE

You fled this island in a bark,
breaking free from my embrace,
your soul shaped like a prow.
The island shrinks daily, the sea
closer by every step on land.

As I walk down the ruin of old blocks
into homes built on dead bones,
I know you were
Ayayughe of the tales,
gathering firewood after every storm;
pounding yam for the little ones.

No doors open where you weaned
a dozen mouths who swung you here and there;
no windows watch the cherry-tree
(its fruits have lost their savage taste).
There all is abandoned,
except the soil God keeps for His testament.

And here I empty this bottle from my travels
over your head; the ocean deepened our love.
Since you broke faith with flesh,
rags sewn to dress you,
I discern dirt piling and piling up
at the beach, the line between us.

In your flitting twilight, you called
my name with your last breath,

and I held you; but you were already
irrevocably possessed for the endless journey.
Today I call your name, *Amreghe*,
with an elephant tusk;
the island vibrates with your music.

*Amreghe was my maternal grandmother who
    brought me up.

BENEATH THE SKIN

Beneath this skin my gods convene—
we frolic on the same, sometimes mean, things
before I follow them to their groves
where they are their divine selves.
There I bathe in the water with which
victorious warriors washed their wounds
to tint my head with courage.

When the warrior-god I rely on
abandons me in the face of a necessary battle,
I take the blame; either I am starting a war
nobody with the veins of humanity can win,
or I have not summoned him with all my faith—
at least, he needs to be roused by me,
and I cannot rouse my herd with one bang.
Who will fight my war for me successfully,
other than the army I have raised and trained
to defend me with my own arms?
I have to be my own general, reinforced
by the exiles and outcasts in my own blood.

Power comes from the roots, from below
despite all the towers erected above us.
And beneath this skin, my gods convene.

I AM GOING TO BE RICH

I know I am going to be rich some day.
The wretch of a road will bring me to a new state,
where I am going to shed my rags for fine robes.
I know I am going to be rich.

I have borrowed from beggars and combed for
        leftovers—
wretchedness has taught me mean things.
But soon my misery will be published for con-
        sumption,
and I will become an instant star.

Then when I fart, it will be a poetic exercise;
if I shout, it will be cosmic outrage;
if I shut my mouth, I will be communing
with superbeings in celestial galaxies.

I know I am going to be rich.
I have never sought the wealth of cash—
I prefer it in kind.
I know I shall be sick of it.

III

The Endless Song (1989)

For Ita

When feeling dictates your line
You step out, like a slave, to pace
The stage, and here art stops,
And earth and fate breathe in your face.
  —Boris Paternak

WE KEEP WATCH OVER THEM

From the scaffold of pain we keep watch over them,
from the perilous precipice of misery we keep watch
    over them,
from the exposed post of lowliness, cold and clammy,
from the slums of existence we keep watch over them.

When they savage us, we withdraw to cabal;
our experience over the ages helps us through—
our women know how to march naked at twilight
and rid the land of tormentors,
our men know how to bury despots with their
    paraphernalia;
we always regroup in the shadows of our fallen warriors.

When *Orodje* ordered us to hold back a falling palm-tree,
he drove us into our closet of metal;
when *Ogiso* wielded his sword against his own subjects,
he fired the guns loaded in our guts;
when the tortoise grew fat as others thinned out,
he stepped into our death-charges—
each praise-song brought them closer to the ambush,
we knew what they loved most and what would
    ruin them.

There's metal in our will, it shows
when we meet hardships—
we do not break down before torturers,
we do not surrender our hope to robbers;
we do not groan despite the daily stabs of hunger,

we do not give in to those who live on the blood
of the poor or the sweat of the strong.

Our will is the iroko tree rooted in our hearts,
it survives whatever storm ravages us;
we can hold to ourselves
and laugh cynically at our tormentors;
we know more than the beasts terrorizing us
that they will fall into a deep hole
as they cavort in our streets.

The machete is our fan,
the rifle our swagger-stick in the dark;
we know what distance to go in silence
before unleashing thunder,
we know how to lead our persecutors away
in the night of their power.
Our will has become our god, and
from the iroko tree aloft our hearts
we keep strict watch over them.

NO PRESCRIPTION CURES
A COUNTRY NOBODY LOVES

And these exceptions gladden the heart:

years back I saw a nameless schoolgirl from Ojojo,
    Warri,
surrender her recess-rice coin to a beggar, one
smeared with the biting indifference of
    passers-by—
even the ant knows the other's stronger need
and brings the millennium closer to a spiteful lot.

The driver who rescues his van from a treacherous
    puddle,
then stops to plant there a red flag
founds a fellowship that deserves universal
    membership—
this rarity gladdens the heart.

And these do not make history or network news,
these do not earn national awards,
these are not sermonizers behind gilded lecterns;
they do not crow on rooftops.
Their gestures are magical in their silence—
the ant builds a monument without fanfare,
the very ant that knows the other's stronger need.

And no prescription will cure the sick country
nobody proudly loves as an inseparable flesh.

Has it ever happened here that the priest offered
    his blood
to stave off the vesuvial scourge he foresaw,
has it happened here that the sharer forgot him-
    self
to raise the spirit of the eighty percent lowlies?

Even the ant knows the other's stronger need,
and no prescription cures a sick country nobody
    loves.

TODAY'S PAIN

Drunk, I believe, with love,
a young lady told her father
displeased with her lifestyle:
"You gave birth to me, not
to my desires;
I'll do what pleases me."
Her mother, who had never
heard this language,
handed her a calabash:
"Fill it with the milk
you took from my breasts."
"But I'll make no demands
of my offspring."
"Hopefully. And you shall
breed stray dogs!"
I desired the lady and
respected her parents
in one breath.
And that's the pain
that troubles my song.

CONSOLATION

I came back from home yesterday, spent
the old, dreary leave routine.
Father was lying in bed, and I said:
"Don't die yet. You know the funerals these days."
"The last I attended was so foul I felt
like not dying, with civil service children," he said.
"And that's what I mean. Don't die."
He declined the naira notes I stretched before
        him,
not looking at them. Colours mattered not to him.
"Save. Nobody knows when this tree will fall;
the winds are out to do damage
with these unending fevers. Son, save."
And there he was, consoled by my visit,
believing that what didn't go to him
would not get lost elsewhere.
We've never been really as close as now, since
my mother left him after I went to school.
Come to think of it, the old man is playing
a trick on me—asking me to visit from far
and turning down my offers, not needy
in indigence. He lives longer, self-supported.
And I end up in a roadside bar cracking bottles,
learning the game of wake-keeping, when
I'll have to go out of myself to swim in Schnapps
performing my duties as the first son
of a considerate proud tortoise.

SONGS FOR ITA

I

So leave it at that, leave it hot on the brazier
that will not cool down once a-burning;
leave it sky-high on the racks
that hands will not reach once erected.
Leave the yam for the beetle,
leave the cassava for the goat,
and brace yourself for voluptuous savagery.

Something is working on me
in the direction of a dance
I have to lead in spite of myself—
I have intimations of a priest
about to abandon the totem pet
kept in his heart
to be savaged by rebels.
I have taken a dark draught,
incandescent, haunting
at what expense I cannot tell.

A strong wind blows within me;
there's nothing to hold to in the wilderness,
and I voicelessly intone the word
to live through the powerful clashes.
Let me yield to love, yield to life
in this struggle beyond me. . .

II

We can now tell, having been born weak,
why we cannot hold back the army within us
with only prayers and resolutions;
we now know, after the trial, that we
cannot wrap the crab with the wide plantain leaf.
We can no longer say we don't sense
the blood of desire whirling in the eyes,
we that find freedom on the road,
in the very veins that keep us fit—
we now understand why the river embraces the
        sea
to dispose of its flood of anguish.
We can now tell, having been born weak,
acquiescent in the light of love,
why we cannot hold back the army within us.

THE BATTLE

For fear of exposing its soft body
the *oghighe* plant covers itself with thorns,
for fear of bad company
the *akpobrisi* keeps distant from other trees,
for fear of falling into the grip of age
the python yearly casts off its skin,
for fear of its head
the tortoise moves inside a fortress.
For fear of our lives
we arm in diverse ways
to fight the same battle.

FUTURE GODS

Ogidigbo, rise
and with your steel
go on fresh exploits—
no longer among the Ijo, fellow sufferers—
to disable the incubuses on our backs.
Let the hands that shook the mahogany tree
break human shackles.

Ogiso, rise
from the moat of slavers' sweat
and wipe out the dust-breathing beast.
Let who conjured a stream to flow in his backyard
water our crops in persistent drought
to stave off annihilation.

Essi, rise
and leave your Itsekiri neighbours alone—
we need each other's love in the world;
raise your army against witches weakening us.
Let the man that bullets tore his clothes and left unhurt
go to any length to regain our strength.

And Shaka, rise
not to devour your own clansmen—
we have had enough of cannibals, emperors and
        generals—
but to eliminate usurpers of our birthrights.
Let who strangled lions in their dens
wrest from our destiny our hidden blessing.

You were all warriors, and never did you
come back from wars without spoils.
Now fight your way back
to help us in these desperate days.
Shame on gods who look on, bemused
as lightning strikes their devotees
in their own groves.

LONDON

Your mouth has been a blade with which you axed away
    my pride
and reduced me to a manikin in your playhouse.
You robbed me at home, then drilled me with mean
    orders.
I have not only been the *Black Sample* to children,
but *Jimmy* to old women, a token species.
Now that I have come to you and seen you at your best,
nude, what hidden charm lies in your scars, moles, and
    eczema?
Cosmetics will not do for your body at your age,
your face already subdued into a bloodless stare.
For all your swagger, you cook with dented pots,
eat with rimless plates, scumtanned wares.
You have no water to wash your face sour from
    inclemence;
your hearth is cold, and your family is dwindling.
The austerity at the palace is unprecedented,
and yet everything from a disused car to a castle is royal.
You have become sterile with age and misdeeds—
your past has caught up with you, and who
will bet a penny on your remaining years?
Your boy said he discovered the Niger, my lifeblood—
who discovered the Thames? Some Vandal drunk with war
fell into your ditch with his danish gun
and came out to tell the world of the Thames.
You are ripe for a fresh discovery, a totem bear in the cold.

(August 17, 1980)

IV

The Eagle's Vision (1987)

For my friends: Ezekiel Okpan,
    Joseph Ewubare,
    and Oladele Akogun

But tomorrow has already been here,
    and we've missed it.
    (Jaroslav Seifert)

Is not the happiness
Of millions more than a happy elite?
    (Boris Pasternak)

NAKED WORDS

This is a family ceremony
to which the whole world has come.
If outsiders understand us
let them imbibe our wisdom and secrets
but we will not change our songs
because of their presence,
we will not sing their songs here
to show that we have heard them
sing about themselves.
Let us not learn from teachers
who have no love for our land.
We must speak the truth
about ourselves to ourselves
without interpreters, middlemen.
Let those who come to us
listen with more than their ears.
This is a family ceremony
to which the whole world has come.
We will be very true to ourselves.

RITES OF INCREASE

Massed on an unending plain, these corn plants
choke the monsters of hunger plundering the
    Sahel;
they incapacitate the beasts that blazed
    a death trail—
nobody was left out unsavaged on their dust-fum-
    ing way.

The earth revives us with this omnipresent green
that lavishly covers the body with long-sought
    love.
The generous sky has offered this facelift
with orgasmic downpours on the heart of the soil;
the womb heaves as contact in the flesh
    generates life.

Let the plough and the harvester be proud
to serve the land. For long shunned, now
    redeemed;
no longer will charities shame my Sahelian fate.
So much growth to celebrate rites of increase.

Massed on an unending plain, these corn plants,
green aftermath of divine love,
choke the monsters of hunger plundering
    my dear land.

(Maiduguri-Jos Road. August 15, 1985)

THE EXAMPLE OF THE SNAKE

(after watching a Tiv troupe)

The snake belongs to a family of demons,
neighbours and outsiders had made me believe.
Till my dark hour in a wilderness of waters, when
I held to algae and was still going down,
held to shadows and was still going down,
held to a log the waves instantly snatched away,
and I was still going down, still going down.
But I came to land across the wide river,
thanks to the water snake, my ferry to life.
The world that did not come to me at that lonely
        hour
says the snake belongs to a family of demons!

(Maiduguri. March 1985)

LAUNCHING OUR COMMUNITY DEVELOPMENT FUND

It was announced in the *Daily Times*, the *New
    Nigerian*,
the television, radio, and other acclaimed mega-
    phones.
Today we launch our Community
    Development Fund
to complete the project the Government aban-
    doned from start
for lack of funds—the Treasury was looted
    overnight
by those elected to generate national wealth.
Dancers are back again from their holes, gyrating
in front of the Chairman and the Chief Launcher,
    millionaires.
The booths are painted bright in national colours.
In those days as dancers twisted themselves out of
    breath
to the applause of the Governor and his vast
    entourage,
we laid foundation stones with party blocks
    that dissolved
with the return of the Honourable Guest
    to the capital—
the budget allocation went with the civic recep-
    tion.
There was no attempt to build what would outlive
    the builders,

and this disregard for afterlife was unfortunate
        for us
Christians and Muslims—heaven could not
        be gained here.
Today, as before, there are dancers to excite
        the chiefs
to pledge millions of naira to build their egos.
Always before new lords that rise with the fall of
        old patrons,
the dancers live eternally digging the ground
        that swallows
the Very Impotent Personalities. And after this
        launching,
the proceedings, the names of donors, will be
        announced
in the *Daily Times*, the *New Nigerian* and other
        acclaimed megaphones.

I BE SOMEBODY

I fit shine your shoe like new one from supermar-
    ket,
so I know something you no know for your life.
I fit carry load for head from Lagos go Abuja,
so I get power you think na only you get.
If you enter my room, my children reach Nigerian
    Army;
so I rich pass you, whether your naira full bank or
    house.
You no know kindness, big man: na me de help
push your car from gutter for rain, not for money
    at all;
and you de splash *poto-poto* for my body when
    you de pass.
To tell the truth, I get nothing; but
you no fit get anything without poor man—
na me be salt for the soup you de chop every day.
I be nobody and I be somebody.

THE HAWK PRAYS FOR PEACE

After my feathers have turned red
with the blood of victims,
after I have converted the moon into a nest
and filled it with the spoils of undeclared war,
after I have seized the arms of the armed
and disabled the fighting spirit of the youth,
after I have become the only bird
and all titles and praisenames mine,
the sole proprietor of the world,
after I have become immortal,
let there be peace.

I AM A BIRD

I am a bird that wants you for a nest.
You can be unguarded and still be safe with me
because mine is the assault of tenderness,
you can swathe me and you in one body
and both of us will still be free.
I am an explorer in an ever-expanding landscape;
there's big game in your heart, enough ground
for elephants to play hide and seek;
at night I can cover worlds with closed eyes.
I think of you as sun and rain—
you have the resources to stave off famine
that now and then smothers the voice with
        parched winds.
I do not want the low haunt of the squirrel,
where he plays pander to the snake below;
they have a mean pact to hurt like witches.
No other place elevates me as you do.
You are the river I want to follow from the source
to the sea—let your current run in my veins.
I want to call from the Kukuruku hills down,
call from the top of the iroko to the desert sand;
I want to sing to small and big ears, open
the closed ones with the gift words of your inspi-
        ration.
I am a bird that wants you for a nest.
You can be unguarded and still be safe with me
because mine is the assault of tenderness,
you can swathe me and you in one body
and both of us will still be free.

FIRESTORM

A firestorm is brewing here, still night
with its coven of death-sentencing owls,
still perilous with blood-streaming rites.
Its direct path is the entire landmass:
it will consume sand as leaves and grass.
The windswept monster is bound to devour night
that has been the terror of the land—
let it burn whatever cloud swallows vision,
the same that keeps the right paths closed.
The storm will pick up wings and wind from
the perennial aches that have become songs—
we are ready to be shaken from the foothold
of hate, ready to part with old habits
and begin anew a season of possibilities;
let's harvest the corn we plant, eat the food
we prepare with the spices of our market.
There'll be room for dogs to love themselves
without eating each other in a cursed trait,
room for the lion and the hare to feed together,
not on the blood-soaked flesh of a victim.
We are ready to give up our shacks
to slake divine anger, ready to shed our old selves
and take on the light the storm brings with pain.
The heat will surely heal wounds that
have refused to go on traditional medicines.
In this African night, a firestorm is brewing
in the brows of a destitute generation, mourners—
let it strike us with a vision of the throughway
to unending days of laughter and love.

V

The Fate of Vultures
(1990)

For my very good friends: Hyeladzira Balami,
Slias Obadiah, and B.I. Abagyeh

I'm not the first to fight; and not the last:
The country will be troubled for a long time.

—Aleksandr Blok

THE FATE OF VULTURES

O Aridon, bring back my wealth
from rogue-vaults;
legendary witness to comings and goings,
memory god, my mentor,
blaze an ash-trail to the hands
    that buried mountains in their bowels,
    lifted crates of cash into their closets.

I would not follow the hurricane,
nor would I the whirlwind
in their brazen sweep-away;
they leave misery in their wake.
I would not spread my ward's wealth in the open
and stir the assembly to stampede;
I would not smear my staff with the scorn of
    impotence.

You can tell
when one believes freedom is a windfall
and fans himself with flamboyance.
The chief and his council, a flock of flukes
gambolling in the veins of fortune.
Range chickens, they consume and scatter. . .
They ran for a pocket-lift
in the corridors of power
and shared contracts at cabals—
the record produce and sales
fuelled the adolescent bonfire of fathers.

Shamgari, Shankari, shun *garri*
staple of the people
and toast champagne;
Alexius, architect of wind-razed mansions,
a mountain of capital.
Abuja has had its dreams!

O Aridon, bring back my wealth
from rogue-vaults;
they had all their free days,
let today be mine.
Cut back pictures of shame
for I know why
    the gasping eagle, shorn of proud feathers
    sand-ridden, mumbles its own dirge
    gazing at the iroko
    it can no longer ascend. . .

Pity the fate of flash millionaires.
If they are not hurled into jail, they live
in the prisonhouses of their crimes and wives
and when they die, of course, only their kind
shower praises on vultures.

PLAYERS

If your king is a born actor,
he will prefer his stage costume to the crown;
he will show up in every theatre
make a theatre of every day
because he loves his gestures applauded,
relishes the flourish of set drums.
You'll pour all the stinking insults on him,
a failure even by the barbaric standard of a king,
but the leading actor won't mind
since he knows that like burrs on a fowl,
they'll fall off when he stretches himself.
He'll not remember his oath;
it was mouthed, he will argue,
to fulfill the inauguration ritual.
Rather he'll flash his toothsome pearls,
a professional practice on stage,
and congratulate himself in the royal media
on superbly acting the demanding role of a king
who failed his seemingly cursed people.
After all, what is he no matter his rank
not to live like his own kind, players?

WHEN TOMORROW IS TOO LONG

And if a juggler ever arrives in town
with an eagle in a glittering cage,
beware of gifts and numbers.
Beware of the season, beware
of twilight and worse. . .

His closed fist presses
a honeyed cake into an ashen loaf.
With his gap-toothed shine for a wand
he throws out one thing
with one hand
and with the same five
takes in more than seven.
I have been a victim of inflation.

And he says
we are born to be beneficiaries
or victims: "you cannot be head
and tail, one or the other."
His attendants, poster-pasters,
frolic in the loot of a flood;
the rest of the world
live in a drought of denials!

If there's ever a juggler in town
with an eagle in a glittering cage,
shun all the trappings of democracy,
do not allow him to perform;
he is bound to be the beneficiary

of all accounts
and you the victim
of that gap-toothed shine of a wand.
Do to him what you'll do
to a cobra in your doorstep:
let tomorrow be too long.

THE PRAISENAME

"Water." That was my Grandpa's praisename.
I don't know how well he knew himself,
but he lived his chosen name to the letter.
He was a drunkard, gulping draughts
of the local brew; so water-logged in the head,
many funny things popped out of his brain.
He covered unwalkable miles to fill himself—
every party needed his presence to be complete
and he was the spirit of cheerful gods
with gourds of fun to share out to all.
As a fisherman he lived on water,
his catch a pride to us all;
a stream of good luck delivered him
silts of fruitfulness, boundless barns,
a clan of children, and an eternity of life.
"Water," I am sometimes called, but I am not;
for I have never taken the cup
of strong brew from the old man in my dream.
And as he recedes into
the darkening shadows of the other world,
I invoke his name, *Ame*, whenever
I see stretches of water, the root
and strength of my blood.

SONG FOR MY LAND

More and more the land mocks my heart.
Where are the evergreens of my palm;
why is the sun of salvation eclipsed
by coups and intolerable riots?

Wherever I pass, mockery of the land;
naked trees flaunt sterile bodies at me—
my blood is hot but not on heat,
the winds gossip loud my dalliance
to embarrass me from washing clean
the tainted face of my love.

Every step I take on the land
is fraught with torments—
my clan no longer contains me;
where I am the adopted son
I am asked for marks I don't possess
before I can be embraced.
I need the entirety of the land.

The song needs the soil
for deep roots and fresh notes;
the land needs the song
to revive its strength
and raise itself.
And what celebrated union isn't
beset by one trouble or another?

I have sat through harsh winds
and alternating hot and cold seasons,
but have not lost my skin;
my nerves are better guards than ever.
I have made love to all tribes
and absorbed the strength of their warriors.

But still, more and more
the dear land mocks my loving heart.

WHERE EVERYBODY IS KING

Come to Agbarha*
where everybody is king
and nobody bows to the other.
Who cares to acknowledge age, since
power doesn't come from wisdom?
And who brags about youth
when there's no concession to vitality?
You just carry your head high.
And do you ask why
where nobody accepts insults
doesn't grow beyond its petty walls?

When you come to Agbarha
mind you, the town of only kings,
there are no blacksmiths, no hunters;
you will not find anybody
doing menial jobs that will
soil the great name of a king—
nobody ever climbs the oil-palm,
nor taps the rubber tree.

Of course, rivalry
has smacked the town
with a bloody face.
No king is safe
or sees himself as really great
in the presence of others.
And they try their diabolic charms
on each other, dying like outcasts

without horn-blasts, without
the communal rituals of mourning.

In Agbarha
nobody wakes to work—
everybody washes his mouth with gin
and sits at home
on a floor-mat of a throne.
Are you surprised
at kwashiorkor princes and princesses,
prostitute queens and beggar kings?
Come to Agbarha
where everybody prides himself greater
than the rest of the world
and see the hole
where kings live their unfortunate lives.

*There is a traditional Urhobo saying that every
      indigene of Agbarha is a king.

WHERE THE NIGHTMARE BEGINS

You are probably dreaming
to go very far in your field,
and you are already living towards it.

When you have gone a long way,
the hopescope will change—
there will be no cowdung to cover you,
no hedges to slip into.
You will then be in the limelight,
the sun-swathed emperor of a vast country.

And there the nightmare begins.
You can always be caught naked
and others will freeze that in their minds—
a photo to brandish before you
when you least need a sore past.

And when you have gone that far,
you become everybody's vision
of a worthy adversary—
you sleep with eyes open
and hands clenched.

You will have to love
the uniform growth
which remained so low
for you to be seen everywhere—
perhaps, an accident; but
don't forget that without feet

firm on the ground,
the head wouldn't be so high.

Upon your arrival,
there's a wholesale offer
of unlimited openness;
and you have to prove others wrong
that you haven't gone this far
only to blow your name into the winds!

TWO PIECES, AFTER A DREAM

1

This thirst
cannot be slaked
by village currents alone.
It cannot
      by the entire Ethiope,
      nor by the Niger.

A calabash
of the Euphrates
and the Ganges
will do the magic.

2

I know the woman
who with a savage song
planted a red grape
in my famished soul.
Someday, moonstruck
I shall shamelessly sing out
to her shamefaced pride
and every other person's
jealous silence!

VI

The Blood of
Peace (1991)

In memory of my father Dafetanure Ojaide
& for my mother Avwerhoke

For the tribe's
sake, the priests cried . . .

(Edward Kamau Brathwaite)

FOR OUR OWN REASONS

We have come out for our own reasons.
We cast fish-nets in the rain to exorcise famine,
we dispatch and receive messages through the wind,
and we want draughts of freedom in the open.
How can we live in the cave of obscurity
and still know the properties of light?
We wouldn't be hiding and seeking
if the world were not a haunted residence.

For us who have chosen to subdue the bull of life,
there's blood in the air and we are not scared—
the hermit imbibes the wisdom of the wilderness
from the wild cherries he lives on.
We are of one mind with the storm
to level the dead woods to give more light
to the evergreens.

What will we look up to without birds
beating their wings above our heads,
what will we look up to without trees
thrusting their arms into the sky,
what will we look up to without the crest of hills?
Our roots drive deep into the soil;
they sustain us in our search for fortune.

We shall return, carrying on our faces
either dazzling prizes or bruises of undeterred blows;
but we would have come out for our own reasons.

WAKING

Suddenly I wake from a nightmare
to the chorus of the wind and birds,
couriers singing songs of the earth.
The veil is falling off the face of the sky
and the sunflower that has been muffled
by a vast dark cloud, breathes visibly
and smiles openly a lovely aroma.
My eyes are dew-glazed.
If we can treat our deep wounds
in the clinics of night, if
the sea of sleep swallows our stream
of tears into its cavernous underbelly,
we will wake whole and strong.

After waking from the nightmare,
I shed tears
for the daybreak of Africa.

YOU KNOW WHY

(for Felie)

We must hum these notes to ourselves,
absorb their fragrance into the vein
to bloom radiance in the face.

I had sung of stars
and thought it was all I could praise.
I had not come to the song of songs.

You are the promised vision,
incandescent flower of light;
you outshine diamonds.

With your light I comb cosmic lanes
for undiscovered jewels;
nobody will be richer than me.

For you I know no bounds,
for you my days long for dreams,
I am drunk in our flight of wonder birds:

the moon is ours to keep
the shield is ours to hold
the war is ours to win.

In another place I would give you flowers.
Here we have lit a bonfire in the heart
to celebrate gains of exploration.

I know how to sing with naked words
but not to sell this prized world
to the cheap eyes of the public

we must hum these notes to ourselves,
absorb their fragrance into the vein
to bloom radiance in the face.

KWANZA

I
The first fruits of the tedious season
blossom beyond the pale of public eyes.
The wind, excited from a spiced carriage,
blows the fruitful tidings with zest.
The savour already fills the palate
with draughts of unprecedented smiles.
Each day adds more gold to the robes
that the land sweated to procure from industry;
each vision is filled with fields of fertility.
Though the yield cannot yet be measured,
the grim army of famine that unleashed sadism
already turns its back and flees—
the bruised land breaks its skeletal mould
into a hand-groomed idol of a hundred million.

II
Those who mocked our naked hands for lack of
    industry
will be ashamed of their ignorance of palmistry,
those who jeered at our play-punctuated warsongs
    as idle songs
will join us in the proud anthem of survival,
those who saw our bonfire as a conflagration of
    kinsmen
will witness the blood bond of our brotherhood
    outlive hearsays,
those who saw a landscape riddled with bones of
    pain
will see the transience of hopeful tears,
those who saw death in the assault of monsters
will clap for the good luck of small ones.
In our time the patient sun tunnels
through mountain clouds and a vast obsidian
    night
into the fresh radiance of a cheerful dawn.

VII

The Daydream of Ants
(1997)

For my wife, Anne, and children

I from backward people still fear God
(Derek Walcott)

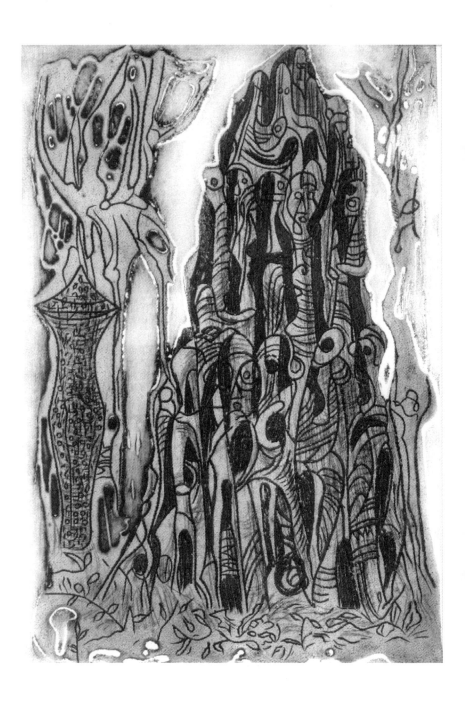

THE DAYDREAM OF ANTS

1
Hunter friend of mine
hide-string this scooped ironwood
through which the wind blows its woes;
hide-string this cylindrical handicraft
into Uhaghwa's music box.

I want to strike hard notes
for the head and hands
that have worked wonders,
and I need to be accompanied
to achieve the voiceful task . . .

2
We are in league with powers
to wreck one vision
with lust for more visions
to refashion a proud world—
with the same hands
that raise a storm of dust,
we paint towers of magnificence.

We bridge craters,
build islands in vast seas;
we have wiped out night
with white fires of fluorescence.
And these are no small wonders,
the handicraft of ants,
a mountain cap over a plain face . . .

3
Man has more than double-built
his manly image of a beast
in the precints of his daydream.
He has torn apart the human suit
he was born with for good;
now an elephant he charges
and tramples the earth—
everything yields to his boots.
He builds monuments out of mountains.
Seeks bridges across ranges
of abysmal gashes . . .

Must he perform magic
to earn the praisename
of the mammoth of an ant?

THE POWER OF VICTIMS

And these are the tolls of dominion:
victims reeling with vengeance.
Cutting through stones to pathways,
arching wide rivers with concrete,
launching dreams to people the moon,
and clearing space for confrontation,
    we strew our way with victims.

And they strike back strange blows,
inflame the land with flu;
inflict deep wounds, leave scabs on faces,
and to be filled take away lives.
They look on as we spend ourselves
and, if we could understand them,
mock us for our creed of greed—
they sacrifice us to their doomed fate.

If we dredged the narrowing Ethiope
for ocean liners to dock in our backyard,
we would drive the mermaid into the sea;
the incensed fugitive would increase
our casualties of drowning.

And the tolls of dominion
litter the wide ways in which
victims wreak their vengeance.

DEATH TRAIL

These
unclad
black
soldiers
scuttling
and
shuttling
here
and
there
hauling
supplies
of
morsels
along
as
the
column
drags
up
and
down
but
advances
will
go
beyond
morning
mist

to
face
the
fire
power
of
the
super
gunner
sun
and
leave
a
rout
and
 a
field
of corpses.

BEAUTY PAGEANT

Polished with vitamin-enriched oil.
Nose carved straight,
lips thinned out;
scars and marks erased.
With a fine point
the beautician fills cracks
with flesh scraped off
the fat dunes of the cheeks.
Rejuvenated with exercises,
doses of lean meals
and vegefruits,
beauty glistens.
With neither scabies,
nor yeasting yaws;
no jigger-cysted toes
and corn-infested soles,
no rites of mutilation;
behold the triumph
of modern magic!
When before now
did a people look
better than their own
gods and goddesses?

AT THE AEROBIC CLASS

My father came alive
riding his rusty bike
through villages of sand
to pay Granny part
of the unending
marriage debt
with a day's sweat.
I can see the old one
accelerating her footroen*,
a grub jerking
trunk and limb
in the daily dance
to give life
an unfinished job.
When I look back,
no obese ant
hauling day and night.

After a dish of
cowpeas and starch,
I drove to the office
to read Achebe's *Anthills*.
I have grown an elephant
without mortar legs
to stand on—
without stealing
from anybody's farm,
I have incurred the wrath
of the *ogbo* curse,

swelling into a pot.
I took bananas
without a forest
to jump from branch
to branch—
who ever heard of
a diabetic gorilla,
or of a leopard
heart-attacked?

I have lost my legs
to Toyota.
The crabs among
my forebears barely
shut their eyes.
How could Grandpa
carry gin in his head
into the upper nineties,
when only one glass
wobbles my feet?
How did Otite
remain forever strong
with his harem,
when one love
chips off my heart?

How do I yank off
this paunch of peril
without paying another
for my parents' patent?

*Footroen is a mock form of Citroen, sarcastic of
    walking.

ON THE WORLD SUMMIT FOR CHILDREN AT THE UN, 1990

1

Warriors raise colonies of orphans
to celebrate their prowess

Players score cheap goals
through bridges of infant bones

Hyenas abolish spontaneous laughter
and make deserts of childhood

Carry no babies, hug none
you legion of summiteers.

2

Children do not smile
they dehydrate in the heat of war games

They starve in the cage of conditionalities
scrupulously exacted by a pack of usurers

They suffer handicaps from basic denials
the allied rich inflict on them

They die in droves in the crossfires
of global strategists

They are the first casualties of wars
politricksters wage to win elections

You mother hens
that destroy your own eggs

You masked beasts
tearing your own brood

You rejoice at your power to double-deal
you who fortify your headships with baby skulls

Children know their worst enemy.

3

Dogs will never shed enough tears
to tell their sorrow,
goats will never sweat enough in a rack
to show the world their desperation.
Babies suffocate from the game
of loveless elders of state.
Disband the cult of masqueraders
meeting in New York.
One can ask for nothing less
for the laughter of children.

VIII

Cannons for the Brave

For Okitiakpe, Omokomoko and Ogute,
who set me on this path they blazed
with songs.

TO ARIDON

To the visionary of time-toned images
I return to gather my share.

To the memory god I return
to imbibe clarity
from his perennial stream

after revolutions of suns and moons.

Divine Sorcerer who captures
every day in its light and dark,
unwind your spool.

I will follow the sure lane of your thread
to cultivate correspondence.

I will follow to the farthest.

I want to rake your gift
from every nook and night.

I will be at the beach
to welcome the waves
you ride through

and be splashed with tales of blue.

I will scale the mountain
for your secret of elevation.

I want your measured rain
to wash off chronic dust
and to bring a record harvest.

To Aridon I must return.

from THE ABIBIMAN SAGA

"Hunter, back from night,
where's your wild game?"
they taunt him
as he drops his bag
of subsistence.
Nobody asks him about
his vision of daemons
and trials with death.

Everyone wants
to practice his craft
on him, and so
the palmist comes
to read his blistered hands.
Abibiman shows faint scars,
which means that his past
was wounded, tear-logged.
But that's not the glory,
the gory epic of victory
that the world acclaims.
"Where are your victories,
where are the monuments
of your manhood?"
they question him.
And none is satisfied
with his silence of an answer.

Abibiman retrieves
from his myths

firebrands of forebears
who knew the sword
but would only slaughter
bulls and not the lame.
From his archives
of oral transmission,
handbooks of business
that would earn him millions,
but he remains human
rather than a tortoise—
to deny himself taint
of evil genius,
he renounced magic;
believing no reforming
will ever absolve the conjurer
from deceit. . .

Sleep has no muscles,
yet it subdues warriors.
Wealth need not be
a crammed self of materiel
but how much human. . .

*   *   *

It's not enough to talk
of those who left alone
might have aged on stone days of nativity
without savouring the spices of progress
or might have leaped faster and further
than a herd of deer in the savannah.
It's not enough to talk

of the night that might have lingered
without flickers of fireflies to see ahead
or the outburst of a black sun
that would have given light
different shades of knowledge.
It's not enough to talk
of deserted forests and flooded dunes,
of plants that might have fruited
in unearthly seasons
or ghosts of known people
who might still have been alive.
There's much more to do now.

STATE EXECUTIVE

"Wherever we dug for safety, we dug into corpses."
   (Donald Hall, *The One Day*)

"Wherever we dug for safety, we dug into corpses."
Whatever we hid in our guts, he found and wiped
   out.
Wherever we fled, he sent his lightning envoy to
   strike us.
We could not shrug off this vicious head from our
   lives.

Shreds of intellectuals hang from branches of
   baobabs,
bones dissolve into the lagoon to assault us with
   bad breath.
We have dug up arms from distant farms
and wondered if the whole Republic were a bone-
   yard.

All the evaporated faces found solace in the soil,
all the spear-tongued critics fed roaming hyenas.
Every year raises the chief's fund of machetes;
winds smother wails and rain washes the topsoil.

From the beginning Ogiso chose cost-effective
   means
to exterminate the bugs that would ruin his rule;
he found beggar hands to implement blood with-
   out stain.

He enlisted assassins from churches and
　　mosques.

For him the long arm of state reaches everywhere
and he circles the land with pointed steel.
The executive wields Aladja-forged axes and rifles,
the human-hooded snake steals in to bite disso-
　　nant tongues.

Thousands of executions prove his inaugural
　　boast
of peace as an array of still bodies,
a cemetery with a busy stock exchange,
a bloodpool chlorinated for a bath.

His rule a great safari of poachers,
a vast ward of diseased consultants,
a free market of limbs flavoured with cheap
　　smiles.
Ogres parade the streets in smart uniform.

Every day lingers with his infinite arm,
everywhere throws up freshly savaged flesh,
everyone yawns from the blood-laden air.
"Wherever we dug for safety, we dug into corpses."

HOMAGE: TO IDIAGBON

We must not lose memory of the rites.
They scared us with savage scars
but elevated us black eagles
with no heights beyond our proud feathers.

Hirelings knocked down the umbrella tree
he planted in the desert,
it had thrived on his steadfast heart.
We know the hell of another season.

Wherever he trod, true warrior,
he made indelible prints
and many drank from his well of steps.
Where are his sure strides
in the blinded corridor of power?
There aren't any nowadays
who will give up their personal estates
to strengthen the poor state.

Do you know now where
they have hidden the wealth?
I thought a little drunkenness
and fidgeting with unkempt fingers
with a harem of girls to toast power
would expose the cache. . .

And the old days come back
to mourn their frightened successors.
We fear insane revenge of the gun.
And that's the strange fate of change,
a smiling sorcerer for a close-lipped lover!

CANNONS FOR THE BRAVE

(for Irherhe)

I knew of no crocodile with his eyes, no leopard
with his stride, no lion with his heart,
and none who exuded such fragrant love.
He always stood in front, foiling stratagems
with his shield of leaves;
he snapped steel knots with his teeth.
He opened his door to the world, gave up
every minute to keep the necessary vigil.
He scorched weeds and clubbed cobras
stalking the flesh of youth—
who was not his child in the thorn-bush of life?

I had sat on his rock stool at the crossroads,
drenched in and out by the dawn bath:
>Let them attack who want,
>I am in a fortress.
>Let hungry cubs lay their ambush,
>I am sure of a safe passage.

And he wrested so many captives from impossible
    grips
that cannibals craved for his sleep to lace poisons
with spices, enlisted hirelings to remove him
so that they could ravage homes at will.
The warrior chief, fresh from victories, fell
in an evening fray; the world earthed his bones.

Though sore, let my tongue fire these cannons.
He put me on the road, impressing on me tireless
    feet.
O Keepers of Urhoro,
open your gates and let him pass;
he walked straight in the crooked lanes of life.
And I know of no crocodile with his eyes, no leop-
    ard
with his stride, no lion with his heart,
and none who exuded such fragrant love.

THE CROW'S GIFT

Crows now fly overhead where there's bushfire—
they delivered the burnt-offering to the gods
who flushed the earth with sheets of evergreen.
I remember their timely vision and straight flight.

How many birds did we break their wings
with the baked balls of childhood foundries;
how many still flew away after we thought
we had tamed them with grains of delight?

When the track dogs of memory
have driven the deer to the marshland,
what happens to the unexpected ducks?
What happens to the fish-ponds
beyond the pale of poaching nets?

I follow birds to their barracks of twigs
where the winged matriarch reviews
the airspace, marks out trails
and beaks out stern orders
to fledging feathers of the dominion.

Memory, I need no sore knee
for my worship; I need your thread
to lead me out of the dark.

I still cherish the warmth of Granny's back,
she deserves fresh cannons from me.
I cannot tell the way to my father's house,

a wide-mouthed python ran to the marshes.
Whatever studs the orphan survives
in the street of public indifference
help to turn him into a lion's bone.
I prefer to fight through every street
than be smothered in the family home.

I know my relations as a fowl knows hawks;
most couldn't be closer without
the discomfort of bad blood.
Today there is no reason to explain
the earth-sky distance between us,
but the discomfitured mouth knows why
it is silent over its scars.

So I always go back but turn from the fire
to where I was refuged like a raw egg;
I have never considered it a birthright
to straddle the blaze of kinship.
O memory, rain a deluge on me.

However credible the creed of adolescent days,
it tears me in one way or another.
I have reconciled to the people
with whom I share the delta of life.
I can no longer laugh without tears,
nor weep without a smile tucked in.

How far back can I see in the dense jungle,
how far can I see through the plains
created overnight out of lost territories?
The genealogy of the lion goes back

to cub after cub that grows into a warrior
and disappears in a den of flawless paws. . .

Aridon, give me the crow's gift;
I need fertile grounds for songs.
And let the vision of scars tear
my pathfinding eyes with smiles.

ENTER MY DREAM

The hush over lingering slavery
drives me to invoke the unappeasable curse.
Let the day break in my lifetime.
Let the Abuja juggler slip
into the dark hole of his craft;
let the butcher walk into a blind knife.

I can only relieve myself in small measures
with ruptures and silent groans.
I summon the energy of the entire body
but my cutlass cuts only a thin goat-path
through the wire-grass of politics.

I have no lances against the hyena's teeth,
no shield against bullets of soldier-barons
other than the deflecting winds of the season;
I have no wand to ward off rampaging boots,
I have no capital to cash on for victory.

If it is ordained for the antelope
to live a full life in the forest of the lion's den,
if it is ordained for the white cockerel
to grow and crow under skies flown by falcons,
if it is ordained for the weaverbird
to sing at the funeral of the hyena,

enter my dream.

IX

Invoking the
Warrior Spirit

For Chris, J.P. and Wole,
    whose songs moved me to also sing.

The lute is but a piece of wood.
Without a heart it cannot sing.

(from Gassire's Lute)

SANKOFA

I

ARIDON, Pathfinder
among visionaries,
clear the forest of clouds
for your bird-prodigy;
let Sankofa pick seeds
lodged in ruined granaries
of ancient cornucopia
to plant in new fields.
A current of charity
washes the land
and questions the
many praisenames.

Sankofa, prophet on wings,
in your crosscountry flight
through the brown forest
that separates the living
from the dead, remember
to retrieve enough dust
for nuggets of lasting joy.
Miner-extraordinary,
flush our days with gold;
demi-god, follow Aridon's
memory trail to its
root of plenitude
and relieve devotees
from neck-deep doom.

Divided, subdivided,
fractured and strictured,
who needs welding
more than the hearts
waiting for binding oaths,
new alliances of faith?

Sankofa, through my notes
I merely translate your beak-
crafted signs to witnesses
of the shameful fall.
I sing, possessed.

II

Multiple scars flash warnings
against legions of divined perils.
Beware. Sankofa says,
        Beware.

Last year we grew enviable yams,
now we grow mere cocoyams.
Everybody can see the change:
the eagle foraging on the ground,
down from lordship of the air.

Now that the iroko we used to lean on
has suddenly grown poisonous thorns,
we see witches' hands in every accident.
Beware of perpetual accusers.
They stole our men and women. Since when?

They stole our gold and gods. For how long?
They fix our cocoa prices. Over our dead bodies?
They glut the oil market. Bad for whom?
They sell us guns to kill ourselves. Whose demand?

Beware. Sankofa says,
    Beware.

There are perils on the highway,
more perils for the small and poor;
there's no smoother course.
If you lose your head in a net,
bite your way out and beware.
Don't drown your memory
in daily palmwine gourds,
don't blind yourself to scars,
don't close your ears to stone.

Amputees, beware of the minefield.
Angola bleeds. Mozambique bleeds.
Monrovia bleeds. Abibiman bleeds.
My neighbour will become my executioner—
where is Osagyefo's dream of brotherhood?
Beware of unknown scars,
lost in carnival bribe.
The monkey drags its tail,
the hen drags its hindlegs.
Lost one ear to thunder,
lost one eye to war.
Beware. Sankofa says,
    Beware.

Snares stare me in the face,
red flags flaunted at the eyes.
Hunger will drive the palate
to dream of poisons as dessert,
blindness will trip the legs
to disable the whole body.

But deafness should not blind
from the market-stampede,
for we hear cries of frogs in floods;
foresee drought in southward drift of egrets,
yet no firm grip of the eel in water.
Hence Sankofa says, beware.

Multiple scars flash warnings.
I am sign-literate enough
in the abstract world
to see the divined legion of perils.
Beware. Sankofa says,
      Beware.

The porcupine foresees a trap
in the night of its rut,
the catfish swallows a hook
in its nightmare,
the iroko hears echoes
of the axe in its skull,
the woodpecker forever
plagued with a boil.

Look behind for the ogre
that already casts a net

over the steps ahead!

Convert. Convert. Convert.
Warrior instincts of the matchet.
Flaring like match-stick when struck.
Killer habit of bees.
Convert to a different industry.

Sankofa, new guard
every light a red zone
every face tinged with blues
every night policed by perils
beware of murderer kins
beware of butcher kings.

Sankofa says,
      Beware. Always beware.

III

Leftovers of forebears
abandoned in the frenzy
of catholic worship, why
should the denigrated ones
not forsake the wax hearts
that are their offsprings?

But nothing so dear
gets lost from Aridon's vault—
the tongue will retrieve
salt lost in the soup-pot!

From the reliquary
of tried hands,
the hungry take up hoes,
body-buiding weapons.
The point's made again—
from one plantain
shoots of a plantation.

If the *tue-tue* bird loses
sight of the catapult's
stone that more than
once grazed its chest,
let no one expect more
than a dirge in the air.

The bell still rings
from the first shift
for new guards
to take over watch,
the land groans;
the cock crows in
dawn after dawn.

"Look over your shoulder,"
Sankofa tells me.
I have looked
at the infinite wealth
left behind,
even as rags cover
tomorrow's holes.

The curative weed invites
to the heart of the woods.

A drum beats from
the heart of the beloved
in the body of the lover.

Memory is
the herbalist of my people,
the forest of
hospitality and hostility.

Sankofa, I cannot climb
Father's tree from the top;
nor can I the thorn-tree
even from the bottom.
Let these scars be
sacrifice for you
to bring from behind
the wealth I need
to survive the course.

AFTERMATH (from IVWRI: INVOKING THE WARRIOR SPIRIT)

Now that we have summoned countless forces
into one body,
now that we have dispersed one formidable spirit
into our multifarious selves
and consecrated into a god the craft
we would like to wield over others,
we can invoke Ivwri to drive harm
from our way.

Ivwri waits at the bottom of the precipice
to cushion us against a hard fall,
Ivwri fortifies the threatened with *utiri*
that blunts the blades of machetes,
Ivwri keeps the gun from firing at his devotees,
Ivwri snatches his favourites from peril
and throws them into safety.

And those possessed by Ivwri, headstrong
annihilate their raiders—
don't try the patience of the impatient;
it is not there, too consuming;
don't raise dust that will be your shroud,
don't stir water that will drown you.
Ivwri's clan of children conjure hurricanes
to sweep open their blocked way,
they raise bees to smite those who taunt them,
they force hostile gods to flee the land.

Afraid for myself at home and abroad,
I have gone to the grove like others
to imbibe Ivwri's draughts, ruled
on the forehead with the sacred chalk.
I have become an irrepressible rebel,
a warrior against myself in the head
as against thousands of strangers.
All the ropes that tied me to myself
have snapped and my restless soles
chase the horizon on its blue heels.

Who is surprised now that I sleep
with one eye closed and the other open
and my people die with a clenched fist?

from EDON: FORBIDDEN SECRETS

 I see women sweating from the broom dance
to forewarn that should I be deaf to the oracle,
I would be swept like dirt out of their sight.
The men forever mischievous in their eye service
hide behind masks of guardian totems
to close the hole should I fail them and fall in.
And the children dispersed from home are scared,
and I have to summon their hearts and guts
to sing tomorrow's anthem with a bold ring.

My people surely have an advanced craft.
No big fish escapes their diabolic net,
they who funnelled currents into their throats;
no animal is too wild a prize for their trap,
they who know how to send a lion to sleep to
        catch it
for sacrifice to exorcise their blood-toned
        instincts.
But if they are the net, can I be water
to slip through their finest weave?
If they are the trap, can I be wind
to spirit through their steel jaws?

Who is deceived by ululations?
If you do not look beyond the paraphernalia
of the high seat, you'll be an incubus
cursed till you topple over into the hole beneath.
If you only call on the people to bow
to your beaded crown and golden shoes,

you will cripple yourself
like the lion of the tales, misdirected.
If you dispenser of the land's produce
trample underfoot the sun in their hearts,
you'll preside over a populace of shrouds.

Let my privilege be a task—
stand in the very front
to deflect harm from those behind.

AKUA-BA

(for Vero)

1

A childless mother draws tears
from the cemetery of her mind.
In her face I see the bed that
the river hasn't covered with sheets.

Even the singing bird that loses its voice
still loves to bathe in the stream
where its feathers will explode into colours
that relieve silences of a dumb creed.

For her who in prayer rubs her breasts with saliva,
for her who sings lullabies to a doll,
for her who in dreams plays in after-rain puddles,
I sing this song:

every womb's a gate—ahead,
an evergreen livery of singer birds,
last fruits of the season,
    so dearly priced.

2

After relief from
the nine-moon mountain,

the gate vindicated
with cries

you'll have to
cut a tree

carve a pestle
pound yam

feed the little one
laugh in your toil

& life will never
be long enough

to savour
before slipping

into the soil!

3

Though
she sleeps not,
still
the nursing mother
more than enjoys
her baby
& motherhood.

(Warri-Lagos. January 10-13, 1994)

X

Nomadic Songs

For Jo Okome & Onookome Okome

> There can be virtues in deprivation, and
> certainly one virtue is salvation from
> a cascade of high mediocrity.

—Derek Walcott

> This sacred craft of ours
> Has existed for thousands of years. . .
> It could brighten a world deprived of light.

—Anna Akhmatova

MORNINGS

Whatever Grandma told me in the morning
always proved true before sundown.
Not just hurricanes that exploded from nowhere
after mornings of sunsplash and no wind.
She was the only diviner without paraphernalia I knew
before tales of Ominigbo's divinity spread from Benin.
"Wait till the sun hurls its missiles at you
and you will understand why I drag my feet."
I always knew her walking with a limp.
Granny went to work her farm at cockcrow,
I followed under the false dawn of moonlight
to pick cherries; wiping my feet with dew,
I earned baskets of favour from the fruiting tree.
As she became arthritic in the day, she pointed
at the vast harvest of her morning's term.
"Wait not to be drenched before covering with an
        umbrella,
fall when getting up will not be a battle for life,
dive when a dip in cold water does no damage."
I know morning palmwine as the tongue's bride
and morning palmoil as the elixir of my gods.
I check my hooks and traps in the morning.
By the time Grandma got to bed, we fired cannons.
She must be dreaming there of another morning.
I have kept my mornings sacred to the diviner.

(May 11-12, 1994)

SCHOOL CALL

The *coocoo* couple wake me
with their duet of love protestations,
and I take my song to the forest.
Looking at only one side stiffens the neck.
I take the trail blazed by fishers
and hunters, my early providers.
I, who lead the iroko cult from a glass home
under the fluorescence of the city citadel,
must go back to the bush school of nativity.
Today I will be washed by dawn-spread dew
in the country of herbs, weeds and barks.
I will be lover again of *uwara*, belle of treedom,
as I taunt *Akpobrisi*, high-handed executive.

This *united nations* teaches me
there's no place without its handicapped ones,
no family without its renegade sons
        and daughters;
none without evidence of Olokun's uneven hand.
Akalamudo, magnate of green, still without a
        shave;
secret of its unyielding shield against warrior
        winds.
Ohohowa with a fortune of feathers, speed-
master of the sky, second only to Lightning.
In the assembly everyone has what to boast of
and a lamentation song even if stuck in the throat.
Look at all the bald ones, paupers
and the craw-craw-rifled bodies

that are invisible until embraced.
Many must be crying to themselves at night.

Today I am scared by the beauty of a snake.
An ant steals through my clothes to sting
    my scrotum
to wake me from sitting on lives that need
    their own rest.
Today the dark-haunting rabbit presents me
a daylight package of surprised vision—
enough trepidation without omens in this
    labyrinth.
I wade through creeks I cannot cut or jump—
I must come down on my feet to the bottom,
not everyone bows to the craft of other powers.
Today I add fresh shades to my song
from this orchestra state of fibre and feathers,
I have been for long a pretender to a high throne
whose anthem I cannot lip-sing without being
    caught.
My body tingles to melting point with the rising
    sun,
I am at once aflame and drenched—
I am a child on the rocking wings of the *apiapia*
    bird
overflying a city where everyone wears a crown.

They are all here, devotees of Sun, Rain & Moon:
legendary lovers on each other's beak
or holed in a rut of green mat, impaled;
clowns, acrobats, divers, sleepwalkers.
They are all here in their *united states*:

cannibals, bald from devouring cadavers;
chiefs and their retinue of grave attendants;
masons building castles to conceal harems;
climbers, cursed as vampires of the race;
magicians changing habit under different hues;
butterflies generously powdering their hosts;
bees armed to the teeth to protect their pool;
crows paying for scavenging with direct flights;
they are all here, trafficking in their trades. . .

I have come home, reprieved
from a self-inflicted sentence.
The forest saves my song.

(May 9, 1994)

JUBILATION DRUM

Panic has caught the invaders.
They have not found the stone
their scouts had prepared for a sling.
"Can stone fly from its known place?"
The powerful are too rational,
the weak commit themselves to faith.

The scouts had read me upside-down:
I marked a missile they would launch,
really the solid shell of a turtle
they saw as an island rock.
The turtle has gone underwater!
Let panic disarm my aggressors.

AMULETS

Light struck me
with a hundred rays,
& I wept loud and blind
before the welcoming song.

I had wandered in the womb.
Must have enjoyed
the borderless soulscape
of the living and the dead,
friends of one existence.
Had wandered in my mother's
space-ship of a womb.
There I breathed bubbles of
Mother's dream of fruiting;
I survived on fatalities of ancestry.
Though in the dark, still
I picked of Urhoro's offers.
What fate as gift now forgotten
stalks every step and heartbeat?

My mouth shut to ramblings
of my expectant hosts.
"Welcome. Welcome, my child"
and powdery white chalk rose
to cling to my velvet body.
Every new-born's a blind
photographer of adult days
advancing towards it.
I don't need to remember,

but I cried, coming into
the house of welcome.

       *   *   *

My faith told what I wore:
incisions to imbibe invincibility,
frothing baths not to be seen by evil eyes;
a cowrie necklace to be favourite of gods.

I procured arms to fortify the body,
the weakest member of my assembled force;
after all, my palms peeled like ripe bananas
and I turned to wield a pen in place of a machete.

What poisons did Grandma see in bananas,
snails, coconut milk and egg-yolk
that made her raise the alarm against my palate?
She meant well to forewarn me
that life's not all wholesome
and there's need for self-denial
of what others covet in their lives—
nothing's good to all, nothing all bad.

At Ibada, so-named after Awo's capital,
I slept outside on nights ablaze
with Shell's gas-flares. Haunted by gods
burning the sky, I sleepwalked
out of childhood into a heated body.
In school bed after an Ethiope dive,
I recited The Gallic Wars, crossed
swords with Caesar and spoke Latin.
Obinomba's dreams penetrated other worlds.

Today neither goat's nor chicken's
blood will meet the oracle's demands.
The cobra grows back its cut-off tail
in the same brush that's our love haven—
we may not reach the clouds
before impacting on the hard soil!

       *   *   *

Fireflies lit my childhood
yet I was the envy of roaches
that couldn't fly except into darkness.
From dawn I was decorated with smiles,
glittering medals, the envy of mates.
The Delta was a cloudless sky of rains
and I saw the sun shine through—
a good sign, Grandma said.

I pinpointed the cricket's hideout
from its needless cries,
discovered how we give ourselves out
by speaking loud in a sign country.
I waited for the smoke-scourged rabbit
at its chosen one of a dozen man-holes,
learned that the fast-witted but pursued
could be blinded by fate into capture.

But these are no small skills of hunting
I learned without paying fees,
thanks to elders who wanted children
to grow out of their iroko stumps.

*   *   *

And I chanted after Grandma,
singer of indoor tales:

Ukerekpe rherhe
jo guo
ukerekpe rherhe
jo guo
ukerekpe rherhe
jo guo.

Pity what dissolves,
yet accepts the challenge
of a water contest
and does not survive
its own folly!

Cricket can rejoice
that Clay couldn't say "No".

And Grandma's tale
still rings in my head:

Ukerekpe rherhe
jo guo
ukerekpe rherhe
jo guo
ukerekpe rherhe
jo guo.

*   *   *

The first corpses that smacked my eyes
chilled with their green uniform.
No blankets in the street to save children
from the horror of their shrunken hulk.
Still, I carried a gun to chase
invaders from the Ethiope's waterfront—
that, after wearing their sunbright amulet
as mine in debates and name-callings!
I would be slave to neither friends nor rivals—
I had no enemy in the sundering fracas.
Only fire could end the dismembering feud.
I carried the hunting bag for Lagos,
it hurt me in the heart that I did—
hordes of ogres took on human habit.
In the front salt-traders crossed
fire to seize riches to boast of,
others buried their faith in mines.
Just another soldier, I threw
down the gun before bathing girls—
war ended for me in that stream!
I carried the gun again, but like
a club in distant lands to kill a cobra.
I can't rest when everywhere's in flames.
The first corpses that I grew up to see
chilled with their green uniform
ripped through by flesh-loving dogs.
Still, I carried the gun in the hunting trail
and it hurts my heart that I ever did.

*   *   *

When Mother initiated me
into the cult of Abadi,
I got neither axe nor machete;
the god would fight for me.
Yes, he fought on my behalf
with my hands, mind and soul;
when I was bruised,
I knew I would heal
stronger than ever.
My god still leads legions
raised from my veins,
hence I am covered
by the arms of Abadi,
my own amulet.
My mother knew from
the shield of leaves that
I would overcome my fears.
I raised a formidable army on faith.
Mother couldn't be more helpful.

*   *   *

In search of amulets
against adversities,
I sought Mammy
underwater.

Underwater
I followed the mermaid
to her mirror-lit palace
and in her tower
offered my heart.

My body powdered,
chalked and perfumed,
I will be received
everywhere a bride—
from the beginning
deference to the bride!

Favourite of water,
I am assured
peace on land—
my piece of yam
grows into a whole.
God will heed my pleas
as happened to Iboje's
& I take home
my share of blessings. . .

*　　*　　*

Hungry,
I went in search
of snails
in the forest,
provider of needs.
I tripped over
a boa-constrictor,
its head raised
and mouth open.
I escaped
the voracious mouth
and stifling coils,

arrived home
without any snails.
I can now live
with hunger
without self-pity
and still forage
heartlessly
for night to fall
and day to break.

＊　　　＊　　　＊

I know two nations, one the source
of the Nile, dying from drought;
the other a silt-bed of crops.
That's me, two generations: the fortune
of one, the other's missed opportunity.

I will not shout the leopard down
for calling me a coward for declining a duel.
Nor will I spit at the sun for raiding me
with heat waves—that will be a futile gesture,
as I am bound to be shamed; I hide indoors.

But I will not snuff candlelight or hurricane lamp
to extend the sovereignty of night,
I will not subscribe to the emperor's divinity
in his naked harangues here and elsewhere;
nor will I beat the drum of conquest.
I will gnaw at the lifesize figure
and bring it to the dust it fouled.

THE LIFE BELT

When did a mermaid drown,
she who needs no life belt
to reach her home underwater?

What swimmer has made the Olympic dive
to pull the river from the bed
in which it never sleeps?

In adolescent days when there was
no water in the pot,
I knew tears from my eyes
would fill it faster
than the mountain well.

The moon was betrothed to light
before I saw her—
now that the couple
multiply worshippers in two's,
I hope to catch the antelope
turn into a bride.

I met her without make-up
in the market,
she led me to the stream—
we would change the world
if we had Olokun's fortune
of sleeping in water
in a gift bed of gold.

I wish to drown.
What animal hides its body
from the bush that's home?
I am in love with the mermaid.
I cannot be happy without tears.
Her bidding is a dive from my eyes.

REKINDLED FIRES

1

From instant gunshots
in American streets
to firing squads still
reverberating in Nigeria,
bullets wriggle through veins
to lodge in my heart;
cadavers litter the mindscape.

Stalked from either side,
I am a hot target
as much in local pubs
as in national brawls—
I wish my armour were
a bullet-proof vest
rather than a livery of songs
with underlayers of light
bound to be torn through
to expose my body!
I am on the line,
and from either side
reports of fatal shots.

2

Freedom is fraught with fear
in my American home.
I spot a murderer
in every smile

spread to deflect the eye
from a handgun.

"Take care of yourself,"
well-wishers tell me.
How does a wanderer
take care of his legs
in Charlotte, a minefield?
How do you live
in the foxhole of the Carolinas
without breathing, eating,
and drinking carcinogens
that translate into fortune?

Homicidal tribes live
in a frontierless state—
in Okpara there is the hag
whose night flights run
against every grain of love;
in the turtle island
the broker who wants
to hang me for profit
in the stock market.
Everywhere they steal
into me—either way,
someone wants to decide
my fate in camera.

Between the succubus
and the slaver, I am
a prisoner with access
to only a fire escape.

And I invoke my warrior-god
to knock big holes
in the vast net
cast to catch me.

SNAPSHOTS ON A WOODED TRAIL

1

These gnarled roots, coiled
pythons penetrating rocks.
Nobody passing here again
will know my pose
with this strange beauty,
nor how I pissed on it
and took photograghs
of rivulets of urine.
Beauty can easily be
devoured and defiled.

2

I love being dark
like this deep green-
leaved cypress that
gladdens my heart
in a soilscape of shrubs
paling before its fortune.

3

This pine has too many branches.
Each branch can be a plant of its own,
big and tall in the savannah I know.
Some are too fortunate in this world.

4

The pine kills its branches
as it grows and advances
to the sky. It leaves only
the topmost ones to survive.
This wizard saves its head
with lives of its own offspring.
No pines in my native Delta
to cheer the old of their craft!

5

The eucalyptus painted
here green, there yellow.
The sun is the beautician.
How colourful to live
in the west! You can tell
the direction of the east
from the beauties you see.

6

These crevices must be
the tree's scarifications.
Every group can be
strangely beautiful.

7

This one so straight
and wears no bark.
Model of the forest,
we deceive ourselves
when we cover, since
lovers want us nude.
There aren't honest
ones like you anymore.

(The Headlands, Sausalito, CA
    May 22, 1994)

AT MUIR WOODS

1

Redwood
rubs camwood
over the body.
A bride shines.

2

Only one
massive root
shoots out many.
African family tree
exiled beyond
San Francisco.

3

A tribe of
only giants.

4

Tallest
in treedom.
Upright,
stretches
the eye's

vision of
lost gods.

5

Trees exercise
human instincts.
Young shoots
take over
before parents
die out.

6

The sun in the forest,
the naira in Nigeria:
in the grabbing,
many suffocate;
deprived, cut off.

7

This redwood
must have lived
with its tumor
for two centuries
of no medication.

8

Even giants fall.

9

Fallen
but definitely
not dead.

(June 20, 1994)

NEW RIVERS

(for Gail Peck, author of *New River*)

A river boasts of fortune,
water covering a bed of sand.
I grew up by the Ethiope River
that exercised charm over the Delta—
a mermaid travelled it to the sea
to freshen herself with salt breeze.
When a student the Niger was my lifeblood
in which Mungo Park's imperial boat capsized
amidst cataracts—discovering a known fact,
he followed the path of carriers to sacrifice.
I shed no tears in college history.

Now I think of other rivers far away
whose flash floods cover the tube.
Mogadishu, Bosnia & Liberia have rivers
whose waves inflict swollen eyes—
there's as much salt in streams of tears
as in the vast sea of governance.
In place of sunlight, shimmering blue
and green that we relish in postcards,
bright red of bodies perforated with lead.
Parallel rivers run through foreign lands,
divide them into left and right.

I came to this world by a river
that brought mother and father from the sea.
With intensifying wails and bleeding,
new rivers have become executioners.

BACKSIDE

The shrine I built in abstinence
taken over by a topless priestess!

Yesterday the oracle cried,
my favourite beauty was a witch
who would steal my talisman and fly away.

The woman I loved warned me against love:
the mudfish I caught simmers with toxin!

I have been wounded by sunbirds
for holding them to my heart.
Be hospitable to strangers,
but beware of robbers.

What I want flashes a warning:
"I'll take away what you have."
I would some day preach
from the rubble of my shrine!

Now I want to be sated
with only the lush of longing.

(November 28, 1993)

DIALECTS OF DIALOGUE

Let us live in mutual distrust.
Since we seek each other's head to prosper,
God help the one not soaked in herbs!
We dialogue in the language of cowries,
exchange puzzles and proverbs,
and assume rattling praisenames.
Odjelabo, here's Ozighizagha.
I am who cannot be guarded against.
You cannot be the Invincible One,
there are higher powers in the blue.
Break my eggs with your sturdiest stone,
I severe your farm from its stream—
we will be laughed at in obscene songs
and there will be no courage to stop them.
If with the bile of your breath
you burned my bridge over wide waters,
if with invocation of cultic words
I poured okro on your stilt-dance floor,
we certainly wanted the other damned.
We struggle to seize ourselves from behind,
though wrestling has become a friendship game.
You want a donkey to relieve you
because you were born to hate any burden;
I want to throw out the succubus on me
because I want to breathe free.
With a burial ground kept between us,
we must live in mutual distrust.

THREE QUESTIONS

1

If you aren't the witch
in the house of mourning,
why are you
the only one
dry
in the rain?

2

You veteran of multiple wars
carrying on your chest
every medal of honour,

have you ever
cried in the rain?

3

You say fish loves water.
But does it,
when the water's boiling?

AT THE BARBER'S MERCY

An egg lodged in the crevice of a rock
O Wind, pass over with your sweepstakes
I seek iroko roots to steady my swaying heart.

There's a riot there of currents
whose phalanges pluck out upright feet—
let the thoroughfare not be my undoing.

I have no patron hunters to scare the hawk
that pries into holes for fledging feathers,
I am the egg the rock wants to spray on its face.

The hide-and-seek game of childhood returns
without the laughter behind plantain shoots,
now the head circles an empty lot
    like a blind bird. . .

Wind flaming to lick the grass I walk
pass by with your armada of sweepstakes,
I have been the moss under a huge stone.

Every step in the hunt demands silence,
I have climbed to the mahogany's leaves
to oversee the entire world from the Delta.

The horses of night know
where to give way gracefully
in their race for time. . .

As the Vulture advances my forehead
into a clearing awaiting the harmattan,
I remain an egg in the rock's groins.

ONE DAY

(for Niyi, after reading *Midlife*)

It all comes one day.
Before I warmed up
to the rest of the day,
I was already there;
forty years in a flash.
I saw no frontiers
I crossed, but I know
I have come to a new state.
Rules have changed—
warnings posted on
different parts of the body.
I cannot laugh for heart's sake.
Instead of pursuing,
I am pursued in the
Hunter and the Hunted
I designed to win
again and again.
It's so far from
the starting point
with its anxious cry—
enough premonition
from start to be wary
of elders' privileges!
I am still a child, but
a fatherless one looking
toward an orphanage.
I have farmed wide

and reaped my own,
patented five crops
for the next century.
In sleep the Vulture
already shaves and
advances my forehead,
but in my country
I am not yet an outcast
as all the bald become.
I dived into changing tide
and came out with a cold.
Unusual, but I am still out
in the business I love.
My head begins to ache
from the morning's wine.
There's no place ahead
to forgive truancy.
It all comes one day.

(May 12, 1994)

UGHOTON

Town that light years would not make brighter!
Always beyond the skyline, lost in the bush
beaten by ghostly hands, I have not found you.
Port or haven, you have kept a forest
of the sea front. You hide a face that
elders would like to touch with a walking stick,
and youths would like to see across seven rivers
from the Kukuruku Hills of their birthdays.
Meteor that created its own niche from a fall!
Kingdom of spiders, school of counsel,
you will always be heard of, untroubled
by the express traffic of tomorrow's hearts.
Market of desires guarded by native palate,
I will come to buy back the wares that
I bartered away when Granny left me, unprepared:
the sunlit face, the rainbows of youth.
Town that light years would not draw closer,
like a bundle that years would not make lighter!
I have been on your road since I knew how to
        walk,
and now flying across oceans I have not come
closer to you; still ahead in the thick bush
that I have to beat with dirt-spilling soles.

(November 11, 1993)

AGBON

1

We arrived home, Agbon,
after fleeing further
than pursuers presaged;
we arrived home, Agbon.
The cotton trees on escape routes
still flourish against sun-stroke,
the *oghriki* trees of abandoned homesteads
commune with ghosts of survivors.

What memory of sacrifice can conjur up
the blood-lit streets of Ogiso's Benin?
What memories of deprivation will
restore nobility to the true heirs?
What possessed wanderers to leave the Cock
for frontiers the horizon held as a looking glass?

2

The file of refugees
trailed me from before birth,
the dust-laden sole of my lineage
returns through distant roads
to the curse of freedom:
flee farthest once you dare Ogiso
and his livery of butcher-lords!
I have abandoned as many homes
as the chieftain broke oath after oath

and turned every foothold into a burial yard.
I have lept from bridge to bridge
built with the sweating hope of nativity
and never sure of home as home.
I have found outside permanent residence
that keeps me from the leopard's claws,
I have fled from companions
who became pursuers to exercise their soles.
The worms martyred in freedom lane
live with cries in my sore heart,
the pilot ants that led us from ambush
still live after dying from the sun's fire.
Craftsmen, they raised bridges over perils;
the *ogbodu* bird stilted to bear pain,
the iguana hastened to alert us of intruders,
and the whistling palm divined for the land.
Who are more saintly than my ancestors?
Out of the multiple scars of flight
names lost and regained, immersion
in the stream that keeps the sea full—
survivors remember a thousand escapes
& live in the fortress of wiles.

3

Once we could run
because there was somewhere
to run to: Agbon.
Now home, we can only stand
and invoke the warrior-spirit.
Home's the end-of-flight.

(Warri. December 31, 1993)

Delta Blues & Home Songs

Terror and despotism are always short-
sighted.

—Nadezhda Mandelstam

VISITING HOME

I have gone back to the spring at its abandoned
    source
to half-quench my burning tongue—
it's in the ruins of old homesteads that
I seek refuge to sustain the exposed head.
Don't leave Mother for good, she shines,
a glimmering shadow of imperial heights.
I have to dig the land into deep-rooted crops
to erect barriers against claims of famine.
I have to gather intermittent produce
into a perennial harvest of hope.
The euphoria of home warmth runs foul
in the universal face of dire denial—
the elders have fallen into the same pit
as their children, neither can raise the other.
This is not the first season that erased smiles,
only to be followed by the sun of contentment.
But who knows when the love of gods
will overcome the connivance of brute rivals?
My fan has caught fire in the heat,
but I recovered my umbrella before the storm.
In this thirst that ravages my soul,
I stand before the homeland's spring:
I can neither drink of its present state
nor will I throw away the calabash—
I must fashion ways to drink of it
without its dirt, drink it only clean.

(Warri. May 14, 1996)

DELTA BLUES

(In memory of Ken Saro-Wiwa and the other eight
    Delta minority and environmental activists
    hanged in Port Harcourt on Friday, November
    10, 1995)

1

The inheritance I sat on for centuries
now crushes my body and soul.

Did others not envy my evergreen,
which no season could steal
but only brighten with desire?
Did others not envy the waters
that covered me from sunstroke,
scourge of others the year round?

My nativity gives immortal pain
masked in barrels of oil—
I stew in the womb of fortune.
I live in the deathbed
prepared by a cabal of brokers
breaking the peace of centuries—
who counts the aborigines killed
as their sacred soil's debauched
by prospectors, money-mongers?

My birds take flight to the sea,
the animals grope in the burning bush;

head blindly to the hinterland.
The sky singes my evergreen leaves
and baldness robs me of youthful years.
These are the constitutional rewards
of plenitude, a small fish in the Niger!

Now we are called to banquets
of baron robbers where space's belatedly
created for us to pray over bounties,
the time to say goodbye to our birth
right, now a boon cake for others.

With what eyes will Olokun
look at her beneficiaries,
dead or still living in the rack
of uniformed dogs barking
and biting protesters
brandishing green leaves?
The standard-bearer's betrayed
& the reapers of the delta crop
could care less for minority rights!

And I am assaulted by visions of
the hangman on a hot Friday noon,
the cries in the garden streets of the port
and the silence in homes that speak loud
of grief that deluged the land's memory.
Those nine mounds woke
into another world, ghostly kings
scornful of their murderers.

Nobody can go further than those mounds
in the fight to right chronic habits
of greed and every wrong of power.
The inheritance I have been blessed with
now crushes my body and soul.

ELEGY FOR NINE WARRIORS

1

The sun's blinded by a hideous spectacle.
And the boat of the dead drifts mistward.
They will embrace the Keeper of Urhoro Gate
even as the soil that covered their bodies
despite guards rises into a national shrine.
Birds that fly past click their beaks in deference,
the community of stars make space for the
        newborn;
they will always light the horizon with hope
& those in the wake who raise grieving songs
will look up to the promise of unfettered dawn,
hope against the rope of the barbarian chief.

2

The butcher of Abuja
dances with skulls,
Ogiso's grandchild by incest
digs his macabre steps
in the womb of Aso Rock.
To get to his castle,
you would stumble over skulls,
stumble over jawbones.
With his ordnance of guns,
a trail of mounds; bodies broken
to arrest the inevitable fall.
Flies buzz round him,
throned amidst flukes of courtiers.

Is the highest officer who presides
over cells and cemeteries
not slave of his own slaves?

3

In these days of mourning
some of my fellow singers laugh.
O Muse, reject their claim on you!

These children who laugh at their naked mother
incur the wrath of their creator-goddess.
They forfeit their kinship, these bastards.

Those whose tribal cackles break loose
as the house's torn with grief
draw on themselves the fate of vultures.

They even ride on the dead
with "Tragedy provokes laughter."
Laughter of the flock of vultures!

They smite the upright ones cut down
in full glare of the noon sun,
Earth and Sky dismayed by the apostasy.

From their corners, they laugh
before somber faces reeling from pain
& mourners can only spit at their noses.

In this suffocating gloom
I turn from my own grief
to weep for fellow singers without a heart.

Only a fool fails to reflect his lot
when an age-mate dies,
& I didn't know there were so many in the trade.

Let no accomplices in the murder
of the Muse's favourite son
think they can fool the divine one.

4

The sorcerer to my shame still lives
as I drown in tears over my brother
he sent away at noon from this world.
The cobra to my shame still lives
as I run from home looking for a big
and long enough stick to smash the demon,
or leave it to suffocate itself with bones.
The world sees the sorcerer's harangues
covering himself with a council of diviners
outnodding their heads in complicity.
He has brought down the eagle
and now plucks feathers off the totem bird!
Does he not know of forbidden acts
that he dismembers the nine eaglets?
He forgets he has left Ken's name behind
& the communal chant of the singerbird's name
rising along the dark waters of the Delta
will stir the karmic bonfire

that will consume his blind dominion.
Surely, that name will be the rod by which
the cobra will meet its slaughter.
The sorcerer to my shame still lives,
but day will surely break over the long night.

5

We'll surely find a way in the dark
that covers and cuts us from those waiting
to raise the white-and-green flag to the sky.
The eagle nests in the nursery of advancing days.
We'll find a way to reach there
where the chorus rehearses a celebratory chant.
We'll make our way in the dark
but would have lost the fear in our hearts—
the dark will not close eyes
to knowledge of stars, dawn and sun;
nor can it smother the message
of good neighbours, lovers and a new country.
No ambush will douse the high spirit
that drives us in the course.
We shall get there
through decades of dark years,
we know we'll have to cross
holes of ambush of hangmen
who do not commit their eyes
to sleep, love and things of beauty.
With the sort of luck we have had
with generals, vultures and presidents,
we'll find a way to reach there in the dark
without government roads and light

but with the rage of being held back
from what we could grasp, stretching ourselves
to the point of exhaustion or death.
None of the survivors will then be
ashamed of being afraid.

WAITING FOR THE NEXT WORLD

Another world is coming,
let those who missed their way in this
wait for the next chance.

I squandered the resources of youth
in family and communal rites,
I didn't see eyes taunting me
from the schoolhouse of my peers.
If I threw the same stamina as I did
upon the oilpalm press upon books,
I would today be a director-general
signing out bounties to my praise-singers!
If as I covered remote farms on jigger-pillaged
        soles
I went the same length with distant learning,
my chapped palms would today be like ripe
        bananas.
If only I denied myself the festive table,
I would be leaner and healthier today;
but fated as I was, I ate with left and right
instead of touching only the right.
I cannot now catch up with the demands
of model figures, cruel regimens.
Obedient to custom, I listened to rattles
that summoned me to the communal shrine;
I could not read the clock on the wall
& today I am too late for the assembly of peers.
I cannot play children's games of speed at old age.
I sought the assistance of beatles

& have an empty barn for my judgement.
I have worked the season inside out, but
cannot build barriers against fireclouds of famine.
As soon as I set my hooks over dark waters,
the blazing moon zealously rose over them
& I caught no fish where others filled gourds
and made proud names with their record catch.
When I worked hard, I sustained
the disease that disables the strong
& I am still reeling from the blow.

Life's more luck than industry,
more gift than sweat
& between tears and laughter
I came out wet rather than dry.
I don't know what my blind choice
has to do with my life!
I must wait for the next world
to be placed on a soft lot
rather than this rock on which
I can break no grounds.
There must be another chance.

(March 3, 1996)

MY TOWNSMAN IN THE ARMY

I would prefer to remain a captain
than the major-general whose stars
Udi flaunts before the world.
He thinks he deserves his rank,
but we know who clears the way
with her body for his rapid advance.
He's risen fast but I do not envy him.
Every year before promotion interviews,
Madam moves from office to hotel,
hotel to office; leaves home for days
and the officer-husband doesn't even
dare ask a question of her absence.
A fool is really credulous. He believes
when she says she's shopping for contracts.
We know what she contracts out!
When the stupid one goes to the mess
for his daily pepper-soup and beer,
he doesn't know others are
chipping away at his right.
The woman enjoys herself, the man
celebrates accelerated promotions.
Most senior officers above her husband
know the detailed contours of her body,
now NAOWA women keep distant from her—
they don't want to be called whores
because of their loose company.
Officers' wives would prefer their husbands
in guardrooms or posted to ECOMOG,
since they don't want them to be infected

with the viruses Madam Udi carries
and gives out right and left to men.
I prefer to remain a captain all my career
than sell my wife for two stars on my uniform.
I pity the husband whose wife is an article
for sale in every Mammy Market.
Some people may be very rich but
their wealth stinks and offends me.
The major-general who has not fought any war
sends his wife to battle in bed with others.
I also hear he loans rifles to armed robbers
who bring him returns from their loot—
let him know what happened to Iyamu!
Udi prides himself as a major-general,
but we know the real general in his home.
I pity the fool who wears two stars
to cover his stupidity, yet remains exposed.
I prefer to remain a captain of my home
than the general whose bloody stars
Udi flaunts before the laughing world.

(Lagos. August 6, 1996)

WITNESS THE FIRE: THREE PIECES

1

The living have stolen the honour of the dead,
their headpieces, busts or full figures
marking streets desolate from live weapons.
There's a dual carriageway to the beach,
execution ground by decree of poachers.
Why on earth will one short-living man
build a hundred-room mansion for himself,
if he doesn't want slaves, djinns and ghosts
to occupy some? The dead must be laughing.

2

I hear the hunter's gun fire—
I am not afraid for the tortoise.
When droves of sunbirds visit the stream,
its water level won't fall even if they have their fill.
Thunder, that stranger to the harmattan,
for all its rumble cannot wake the dead.
Let the tsetse-fly stalk the tortoise,
it will abandon its ambush; hungry.
Nobody yet to boil stone into yam.
I am Akalamudo, tropical evergreen;
I pale before none. Look at me:
I am not afraid of your face or fire.

3

The street is a burnt offering.
Times have changed without love.
Small ones smaller than ever in the fray
but have not been swallowed in the clouds,
only they cannot go far on roads built
to bring them out to work and back home.
There's a shortcut to the cemetery,
now advanced into distant farmlands;
hunters dead beside their dogs and guns—
the warlord rattles the airspace with decrees.
A few antelopes stand on elephants and leopards
but the majority lie crippled by intolerance.
A child's born but has not been named
by parents not sure of seeing the next sun.
The wind still blows, the sky overcast. . .

(Reading, PA. October 11, 1996)

Glossary

Abadi   one of the Urhobo gods of war.

Abibiman   Akan for land and people of the African world.

Abuja   Nigeria's new capital.

Agbon   my native clan in Delta State, Nigeria.

akalamudo   an evergreen tall tree.

akua-ba   Akan figurine ("fertility doll") used to induce pregnancy or the birth of fine babies.

akpobrisi   a mythical tree with mystical powers. It is believed that akpobrisi, a tyrannical tree, surrounds itself with only weeds.

Aladja   town near Warri and site of an iron and steel complex.

Alexius   fictional name but meant to recall first name of a Nigerian political leader of the early 1980s.

Ama hirhe erherie   Urhobo for a turn in fortune like when the pursuer becomes the pursued.

Amadiora   god of thunder among the Igbo people of Nigeria.

Ame   Urhobo for Water, the praisename of my grandfather.

apiapia   high-flying tropical bird of the falcon family called so in Urhobo after its familiar sound.

Aridon   god of memory and muse of the Urhobo people.

Aso Rock   Presidential Mansion in the Nigerian capital of Abuja.

Awo   Chief Obafemi Awolowo, first premier of Western Region of Nigeria.

Ayayughe	selfless mother in Urhobo folklore who denies herself food and other necessities in order for her children to be filled.
calabash	a traditional vessel made from a gourd.
Chukwu	Igbo for God.
coocoo bird	named after the sound it makes.
ECOMOG	military unit made up of officers and men from various West African countries, including Nigeria and Ghana, responsible for order in war-torn Liberia.
Edon	traditional institution in Ughelli, probably derived from Uselu of ancient Benin, where would-be kings are trained on the do's and don'ts of rulership. The student prince has to spend three lunar months confined to a secluded house by which former rulers were buried. Throughout this period, he is forbidden from

175

sleeping with a woman or indulging in sumptuous dishes. Elders, priests, priestesses, and chiefs give him lessons about taboos and service. There he learns the different sacrifices he must make to be in good standing with his gods and people. Before he gets installed as king, he watches the women perform the broom dance, the symbolic importance of which sinks into his head.

Egba   local Urhobo god of war served with dog sacrifice in Kokori.

Eloho   Urhobo women's sect of fertility rites. Name of my daughter.

Eshu   Urhobo for the god of evil.

Essi   Warri chieftain and warrior of Igbudu quarter.

Ethiope   river that for the most part separates Delta and Edo States.

garri	staple food from cassava roots.
Ibada	the village in the Delta part of Nigeria, named after Ibadan, in which my grand-mother raised me.
Iboje	founding igbe religion chief priest, a Kokori native.
Idoto	water goddess and muse in Okigbo's Heavensgate.
iroko	sacred Urhobo tree. Sometimes served as god of wealth.
Ivwri	battle-god created and invoked by Urhobo people during the slave-raiding period. Ivwri was then invested in a carving, part human, part animals with many icons that defined the fighting spirit of the people. The god is offered a com-munal animal, any healthy and robust animal seized by the priest and not paid for. The worshippers of Ivwri

succeeded not only in defending themselves against the enemy who saw them as trees as they macheted them, but also recaptured some of their people already enslaved. This feat is remembered in the art work which has survived that period to this day.

Iyamu   A Nigerian retired police inspector who was executed for abetting a series of armed robbery in the Benin and Delta areas.

kolanut   nut from the kola plant popular in West Africa. In pidgin, it designates bribe.

Kwanza   in Kiswahili means the first fruit.

kwashiorkor   Akan word now English for protein deficiency that causes protruding stomachs in children.

Kwokori   young man of the Kwokori family in Ekpan, Ovu, who died about 1975 in an acci-

dent. He was very national-
istic.

Kukuruku Hills | in the northeast part of Edo
state, Nigeria.

Lagos | old capital of Nigeria and
still the commercial centre.

madras | the dress fabric called
"wrapper" used by men and
women in the Delta area of
Nigeria.

Mammy | mamiwata, mermaid, wor-
shipped by igbe sectarians.

mammy market | market in military barracks
in Nigeria.

Mowarin | native of Ikweghwu,
Agbarho, who was very
influential in Urhobo poli-
tics. I am named after him,
hence I call him my name-
sake.

naira | Nigerian currency.

NAOWA | Nigerian Army Officers'
Wives' Association.

Niger	major West African river whose delta in Nigeria is the poet's home state.
Obinomba	I attended St. George's College, Obinomba—a Roman Catholic secondary school.
Odjelabo	praisename of Okitiakpe. It means the "Invincible."
ogbo	a charm tied to a farm or fruit tree against thieves who would have swollen bellies should they defy its presence and still steal from the farm or tree.
ogbodu	stilt-legged riverine bird from which the ikenike stilt-dance derives.
oghighe	soft tree with thorns.
oghriki	ritual tree planted at the centre of a new settlement by its founders.

Ogidigbo	Urhobo warrior who terror-ized the Ijo people.
Ogiso	literally means "king of the sky." Benin monarch and dynasty whose tyranny drove the Urhobo out of the kingdom to their present delta home.
Ogun	Yoruba god of iron.
ohohowa	high-flying tropical bird named by the people after the sound it makes.
Okitiakpe	great udje poet and per-former of Ekakpamre.
Olokun	god/goddess of wealth and beauty.
Ominigbo	legendary diviner of Benin who foretold the coming of British invaders on a specific day at noon in 1897. However, as noon passed and the British were not seen, the Oba ordered his execution for lying and frightening him. As the executioners complet-ed their task, the British sol-

diers appeared, enacted the Benin massacre and deported Oba Ovoramwen to Calabar.

Orodje — traditional ruler of the Okpe people in the Delta area of Nigeria.

Orogun — town and clan that hold the iguana sacred.

Osagyefo — Title of Dr. Kwame Nkrumah of Ghana; literally the Redeemer.

Osonobrughwe — Urhobo for the Supreme God.

Otite — Okpara patriarch known to have married uncountable wives and famed to have the largest number of children in all Urhobo. He lived very long.

Ozighizagha — a praisename which suggests terror—one who is not to be toyed with.

poto-poto — pidgin for muddy water.

Sango	Yoruba god of thunder.
Sankofa	Akan mythical bird with its beak looking backward, symbolic of going back in time and bringing to the present past values needed now.
Saro-Wiwa	renowned writer, Ogoni/Delta minority and environmental activist, who was framed and hanged with eight other activists on Friday, November 10, 1995.
Schnapps	a brand of imported gin popular among old Urhobo people.
Shamgari, Shankari	meaningless names but suggesting an important Nigerian political leader of the time.
soldier-ant	also called army-ant and driver-ant.
Tee Es	T.S. Elliot, modern American-born British poet.

Tiv
an ethnic group in Benue State of Nigeria known for their suggestive dances.

tortoise
the land turtle imbued with myths of a trickster animal. Most times, it is caught and shamed.

tue-tue
very small and cunny bird that makes that sound and leads on the hunter into the wilds.

udje
a performance of songs of abuse and dance for which Ujevwe and Udu clans of Urhobo are renowned.

Ughoton
Bini town on the Benin River which was considered very distant from Urhobo in ancient times.

Uhaghwa
god of songs and performance, symbolised by a feather. Uhaghwa, also a muse, possesses the performer, singer, and dancer to perform wonderfully and be applauded.

Ukerekpe rherhe jo guo   song from a folktale in which block of clay and cricket argued about seniority and God asked them to swim across a stream to settle the dispute. Block of clay dissolved and lost the contest.

Urhiapele   god and town named after it by the Ethiope river-front. Corrupted by the English to Sapele.

Urhoro   the most pervasive philosophical and existential concept in the Urhobo world. "You make your choice at Urhoro and live your life according to that choice," the saying goes. It is possible in life, according to elderly mystics, to change a hard fate with sacrifices of atonement. People leave the spiritual world through Urhoro to be born and upon death go back through there to start the spiritual existence. Life is cyclic and there is movement on a continuing basis from material

	to spiritual and vice versa. Urhoro has come to embrace destiny and fate.
utiri	traditional medicine that deadens sharp objects from cutting who uses it.
Uvo	mythical Ujevwe (Urhobo) warrior whose mystical power was violated by a woman who lured him to sleep with her and she urinated on his charms, which made them lose their potency.
uwara	slender tree that is said to be beautiful. Represents the female principle and is the only tree that can grow in the same place as the tyrannical akpobrisi tree.